FOREWORD

If the arts are to continue to flourish and to be enjoyed in this country a sound infrastructure of buildings for the arts is vital. Well designed theatres, concert halls and exhibition spaces, and buildings which are sensitively converted, enhance our experience of the arts - the design, acoustics, lighting and way that a space is used within a building to present a performance or objects inevitably affect our perception of what we see or hear. As the millennium approaches it is specially important that the fabric of our arts buildings should be in the best possible order, ready for the 21st century. There are many fine buildings to conserve; new ones are being built. During the 1990s the Council will help to sustain and develop the building infrastructure through its feasibility studies scheme that gives grants towards the cost of feasibility studies for arts buildings, and a capital incentive scheme that is being prepared for launch in April 1991. *The Arts Council Guide to Building for the Arts* is a handbook of practical help for people planning to build for the arts - new buildings, conversions, adaptations or refurbishments - who have no specialised knowledge of the process. It contains a wide range of fundamental information, as well as suggestions about where to find more detailed guidance. It is the first such book to be written about arts building in Britain and I hope that it will be welcomed as an extremely useful source of advice.

P G Palumbo
Arts Council of Great Britain Chairman,
16 May 1990

1

HOW TO USE THIS BOOK

This book is divided into three sections:

SECTION 1: The Process

This section gives an overview of what is involved in a building project - from the development of the initial idea to the opening of the building.

SECTION 2: Specifics

This section fills in the details giving back-up information, guidance notes and checklists on a range of subjects related to building for the arts. It can be used as a reference at any stage in the process outlined in the previous section.

SECTION 3: Design requirements

This section gives information about the requirements of buildings and spaces within buildings which are designed to house the arts. It is intended to be used as a general guide to the initial planning of an arts facility.

Each section has an introductory chapter outlining the scope and contents.

There are also five appendices listed below.

CONTENTS

LIST OF ILLUSTRATIONS

ACKNOWLEDGEMENTS

This book could not have been written without
the help of many individuals and organisations.

Arts Council and Regional Arts Association
Officers have provided advice and information on
a wide range of specialist topics. The members of
the editorial committee (Bill Dufton, Director of
Southern Arts; Roger Jefferies, Chief Executive of
the London Borough of Croydon; Rick Welton,
Director of the Arts Development Association)
have overseen the whole project.

Additional help has been given by: architects
Roderick Ham, Timothy Ronalds and Nicholas
Thompson; theatre consultants Peter Angier,
Richard Brett and Iain Mackintosh; and by Ian
Reekie, Scunthorpe Borough Leisure Services
Officer. The National Centre for Voluntary
Organisations, the Policy Studies Institute, the
Directory of Social Change, Planning Aid for
London, the Royal Institute of British Architects
and Butterworth Architecture have all proved to
be valuable sources of information and have given
permission for some of their material to be used
in this publication. Arts organisations throughout
the country have sent information about their
buildings and many architects have provided photographs and drawings. Tech Computer Office,
Richmond, helped produce the text and organise
the information. The diagrams of theatre layouts
were drawn by Mark Thompson.

1 THE PROCESS

The design and planning of any building project is a complex process. This is particularly so for arts buildings, which have to meet exacting technical requirements as well as respond to the various and sometimes conflicting needs of artists and performers, the people who use the building, funding organisations and the general public. In building for the arts, there are no off the peg solutions or standard instructions to be followed. As with any creative process, the initiation, planning and design of an arts project involves exploring possibilities, assessing options, establishing priorities, accepting compromises and taking informed decisions.

Before any building work can start, a detailed design has to be drawn up. Before a design can be prepared, the requirements, in terms of spaces and facilities, have to be defined. To define these requirements the uses to which the building is to be put and the activities it is to house, need to be established. These can only be worked out by going through a period of research and evaluation. This is the starting point for the building project.

There is a wide range of people and organisations involved in the provision of buildings for the arts, and the initiative to build can come from a number of different sources. They include:

- artists and arts companies looking for new or improved accommodation;

- local interest groups seeking to provide spaces for the arts in their areas or to find a use for an attractive building;

- public authorities aiming to improve facilities for their local communities;

- development bodies looking to the arts to provide a social mix in redevelopment projects;

- educational and other organisations wanting to make arts provision for their students and user groups or to expand existing provision to attract a wider use.

Each of these groups starts from a different position - as their areas of interest differ, so will their objectives. This means that they have to follow different routes to achieve their objectives. During the planning stages a number of key elements - the arts provision, the site or building and financial resources - need to be brought together before any design work can begin. Some organisations will have one or more of these elements defined at the outset. For example, a developer may have a site available while a theatre company, looking for a new home, will know what it wants to do in terms of the arts.

By the time these different groups have reached the stage of drawing up the brief (the set of instructions on which the design for the building is based) they will be on common ground as the process of working with the design team and the design and construction of the building follow a standard pattern determined to a large extent by the working practices of the professional groups involved.

Because of this diversity of approach, the early parts of section 1 only give an overview of the processes to be followed in defining and developing the key elements, while section 2 sets out more detailed information under the three main headings 'Arts and Venues', 'Sites and Buildings' and 'Finance and Funding'. Information on the design of spaces and facilities for the arts is given in section 3, 'Design Requirements'.

In practice, many of the processes outlined in 'Getting Organised' and in 'Drawing up and developing a proposal' have to be carried out simultaneously, with the initiating group alternately moving forward with its research and evaluation and taking the appropriate practical initiatives as these become necessary. 'Getting Organised' is placed first in the text only because some of the matters may take a long time to be resolved.

GETTING ORGANISED

The Regional Arts Associations provide a valuable source of advice and information throughout the whole planning process, so it is important to consult them at a very early stage. From April 1991 the RAA's will be replaced by 10 Regional Arts Boards.

While the initial research work is being done, a number of practical measures have to be taken to ensure that the initiating body is properly constituted to undertake a building project, that it has the necessary expertise and financial resources to carry out the work and, most importantly, that there is a suitable site or building available.

There is no specific stage in the process when any particular measure has to be taken. It is up to each individual organisation to make an assessment of when it is appropriate for it to formalise the organisation, exchange contracts on a site or building, launch a fundraising campaign, etc. But it is inadvisable for a project to proceed to the briefing stage without these matters being satisfactorily resolved.

SETTING UP AN ORGANISATION
Where no organisation exists, one will need to be set up. An 'ad hoc' group of people may work together quite acceptably at the very early stages when the project is first being discussed and initial ideas are exchanged. Once this group begins to consider appointing staff or consultants, or to explore the possibility of acquiring a building, it needs to be constituted on a proper legal basis.

An existing organisation also has the option of setting up a separate organisation to oversee the building project. The completed building can then be handed over or leased back to the initiating organisation as appropriate.
(See Section 2 page 37.)

DEFINING OBJECTIVES

The way a group is constituted needs to relate to the purpose it is to serve. Its aim may be:

- to act as a co-ordinating or pressure group, defining what is needed, exploring the possibilities, bringing together interested parties and encouraging other organisations to provide the necessary facilities;

- to plan, fund and carry out a building project, with the intention of handing over the building to another organisation (e.g. a theatre company) once it is completed;

- to plan, fund and carry out a building project, with the intention that it will remain the property of the originating organisation, but will be leased to an arts organisation which will use the building on an agreed basis;

- to complete a building project for the organisation's own use.

TYPES OF ORGANISATION

The main legal formats are:

- a club or association. This can only be considered as a possibility for the first of the above situations as a group constituted in this way cannot hold property in its own right;

- a co-operative society. This is only appropriate where all members of the group have an equal interest in and responsibility for the building (e.g. a group of artists looking for studios or dancers looking for rehearsal space);

- a trust. Many arts centres and arts buildings which buy in work (e.g. by promoting a touring company production) are managed by trusts. This format can also be used where a separate body is set up to oversee a building project;

- a company limited by guarantee. This is the basis on which most producing companies in the arts operate. (e.g. regional theatre companies). A company limited by guarantee differs from the company limited by share holders (the basis on which most commercial businesses operate) in that it has no shareholders and cannot distribute profits to its members. Its activities are regulated by the Companies Act.

REGISTERING AS A CHARITY

Whichever way an arts organisation is constituted, the question of charitable status should be considered, as there are a number of advantages to be gained. These include tax concessions, mandatory rate relief and eligibility for certain forms of grant aid.

An organisation can only register as a charity if it is established for charitable purposes. These purposes are defined by law. Most arts activities fall within one of the categories which are deemed to be charitable.

While the process of registering a company is comparatively quick, the time between the submission of an application to the Charity Commission and the receipt of final consent by the Commission and the Inland Revenue can range from a few months to a year or more.

Note: The Charity Commission has jurisdiction in England, Wales and Northern Ireland. In Scotland charitable status has to be cleared with the Inland Revenue Claims Branch.

SOURCES OF INFORMATION

Specimen sets of Articles of Association and Memorandum of Association for a company limited by guarantee for undertaking artistic activities are available on request from the Information Offce at the Arts Council. These provide a standard format for setting out the purposes for which a company is established and the basis on which it operates.

The Legal section of the National Council for Voluntary Organisations provides guidance on the process of applying for company and charitable status. A moderate fee is charged. The NCVO also publishes a number of guides on the formation of charities and liabilities of trustees, etc. The address is listed in the Directory section.

The Charity Commission publishes information on how to apply for registering and on the Charities Act 1960 which set up the Central Register of charities.

When setting up a company or trust it is advisable to contact a solicitor with experience in this type of work.

APPOINTING A CO-ORDINATOR

Only in a small and relatively simple project can the co-ordinator's role be carried out by an arts administrator who has a company or venue to run, by a local authority officer who has a range of other duties, or by a member of the board working on a voluntary basis in his/her spare time. Once the detailed work begins, somebody has to make the administration of the project his/her full-time job, or, at the least, his/her overriding priority. In many cases, this supervisory role will need the support of a team of people with a range of skills.

Although at this stage the building could be several years away from its opening, it is worth giving some consideration to whether any staff appointments should be made. Provided the project continues without any major interruptions, there could be sufficient work to keep the co-ordinator fully occupied until the building opens. There are advantages to appointing the director designate to research and draw up the programme and write the brief. The approach is likely to be more practical, if the person undertaking this work does so on the basis that he/she is going to be responsible for running the venue when it opens. A disadvantage is that he/she may define the brief too closely to his/her own particular interests and then leave when the building opens.

THE SKILLS REQUIRED TO DO THE JOB

Co-ordinating a building project is a demanding job. It needs someone who is able to:

- communicate effectively both in talking to people and in writing. The job involves explaining the proposals to those who will help finance it, presenting it to the media and the public, negotiating with the funding bodies, making grant applications, briefing consultants and writing the design brief;

- take decisions. Planning an arts facility is a process of exploration and evaluation. In order to progress, some options have to be selected and others abandoned. However much advice is taken, the ultimate choices lie with the initiating organisation. Many will be matters of judgement;

- work with other people. Building an arts facility draws in people with a wide range of interests and skills (e.g. artists, architects, bankers, construction workers). Anyone co-ordinating an arts project needs to be flexible in their approach and able to incorporate other people's views into their thinking;

- plan effectively. A building project extends over a long time period. It involves a number of interdependent processes which have to be developed simultaneously if it is to progress;

- be financially aware. Building projects involve large sums of money which have to be organised to get the best returns and be available when they are needed. An ability to think strategically is required as well as the more basic book-keeping skills.

SELECTING CONSULTANTS

Various consultants may need to be brought in to advise on different aspects of the project in the early stages. These will, in the main, be short term appointments to meet specific needs.

Before any design work can start, the architect and/or design team need to be appointed. It is advisable to think about these key appointments while the proposal is still being developed to allow adequate time for selecting the right people for the job. In certain situations, it is worth appointing some members of the team to advise on the development of the proposal. For example, a theatre consultant can advise on what type of facility is best suited to an area, while an architect can help assess the suitability of a particular site or building for conversion.

See the chapter in Section 2, 'Working with Consultants'. Information on the design team is given on page 18.

FINDING A SITE OR BUILDING

The search for a vacant site or an existing building which offers potential for conversion, can be a major undertaking. Location is an important factor, as is accessibility. Good sites are not easy to find, especially where they need to be centrally located. This is often a decisive factor in so many arts organisations choosing to convert redundant buildings rather than design and build from new.

Before starting the search for a site or building, it is advisable to make a list of basic requirements and grade them in terms of priority (e.g 'essential', 'important' and 'desirable'). The main characteristics of possible sites and buildings can then be detailed and compared with the checklist of requirements. This is not a system for selecting a site or building, but it can help to concentrate attention on the possibles rather than spending time assessing those which have some characteristic which makes them basically unsuitable.

Detailed information on this subject is given in Section 2 in the chapter on 'Site and Buildings'.

GENERATING SUPPORT

An arts building has to satisfy a wide range of people: those who work in it, those who use it,

Street event to generate support for the Norwich venue campaign
(photograph by Peter Smith)

those who help to pay for it and even those who pass by and look at it. There is also a negative component to be considered: those who think the money should have been used for something else, those who wanted the site or building for another purpose, and those who oppose any new initiative.

The amount of opposition tends to be diminished when people understand what is proposed and feel part of it. Local arts, community and environmental groups need to be consulted and given a role if they express an interest. Organisations which are going to be approached for funding, either for the building or the subsequent activities, should be consulted at an early stage.

Any project which becomes a political issue faces a difficult future, both in getting off the ground and later when it is open and running. It is worth trying to avoid this by identifying the individuals in each group or political party who have an enthusiasm for the arts or for the particular project proposed. They will be able to advise on how best to present the project and will be in a position to talk about it to their less enthusiastic colleagues, to get across the board support.

It is not always necessary to present all the facts

to all the people with the same degree of emphasis. It can be more effective to work out what aspects are likely to appeal to the different interest groups, and stress these in the initial discussions.

Where a project faces strong and potentially damaging opposition, a public relations consultant may need to be brought in to advise on how the problem can be tackled.

PLANNING A FUNDRAISING CAMPAIGN

Whenever possible, it is advisable to try to raise the money for the initial work through a single grant or donation, saving the general fundraising campaign for the major appeal.

When the appeal is launched, it is important that it is soundly based and that the figures can be substantiated. The necessary information may only be available once feasibility studies and development studies have been completed but the campaign can be planned in outline well in advance. This will enable it to be launched as soon as the more detailed information is known.

There are often long gaps between funds being committed and the money being paid - for example, much of the income from fundraising will be in the form of covenants, spread over a four year period. It is therefore important to get the fundraising campaign launched well before the major expenditure is incurred.

(Further information on fundraising is given in Section 2 in the chapters 'Finance and Funding' and 'Working with Consultants'.)

DRAWING UP AND DEVELOPING A PROPOSAL

Building is one of the few remaining areas of activity where the product is individually designed to meet the specific requirements of the commissioning organisation. If the completed building is to operate successfully, these requirements need to be carefully defined and communicated to the designer.

In other areas, those who wish to avoid this process can opt for a purpose built facility (e.g. a unit on an industrial estate or space in a commercial office block). There are no 'arts estates' or speculatively built performance spaces and art galleries, so those seeking to provide facilities for the arts have to spend time working out exactly what sort of building they need.

This involves defining the initial ideas, evaluating the various options, testing their feasibility and working out a detailed proposal on which the brief can be based.

TYPES OF STUDY

The term 'feasibility study' is often used to describe any exploratory work undertaken in the pre-design stages. In fact, any one of several different types of studies could be required.

Research studies are undertaken at the beginning of the planning process to collect information and define the options.

Strategy studies explore the options, look at alternatives and define directions.

Feasibility studies are carried out during the second stage to test whether a proposal is technically and/or financially viable.

Development studies work out the detailed proposals. They should only be undertaken once the outline proposals have been tested.

WHO DOES THE WORK

How these studies are carried out depends on the size and complexity of the proposed scheme and the resources of the initiating organisation. The work can be undertaken by:

- the project co-ordinator, with professional advice on specific aspects;

- a number of individual consultants commissioned to carry out separate studies at different stages in the process;

- a single consultant appointed to carry out the whole of the initial planning and testing, through to the preparation of the brief.

(See the chapter in Section 2 on 'Working with Consultants'.)

PUTTING TOGETHER A PROPOSAL

This first stage can be seen as one of finding out the answers to a series of questions, with the objective of drawing up a proposal in sufficient detail to give a broad outline of what is required.

Not all these questions will be relevant in every case as many arts projects start with more limited options.

WHY BUILD?

The reasons for considering a building project need to be identified and assessed. The motivation could be one of need or of opportunity. Even where the need appears to be obvious, it is worth asking whether building is the only valid response to the situation.

LOSS OF EXISTING FACILITY

In some cases, existing facilities cease to be available. This can come about through redevelopment, the end of a lease or the deterioration of the building to such an extent that the cost of renewal is prohibitive. Facilities which are lost in this way are rarely replaced by exactly the same sort of provision. The enforced change provides an opportunity to assess future needs and respond accordingly.

GAPS IN PROVISION

There are still some areas of the country which have no facilities for the arts and others where there is no provision for a particular art form or scale of production.

For instance, good facilities for dance are lacking throughout the country, as are adequate rehearsal spaces for all the performing arts. Halls suitable for chamber music and recitals are limited. Many towns and cities have little provision for the visual arts, particularly those in which the public can participate. Contemporary and technologically based forms of expression in both music and the visual arts are often ignored. There are very few spaces dedicated to the presentation and development of Afro-Caribbean and Asian arts or to the work of artists from these communities.

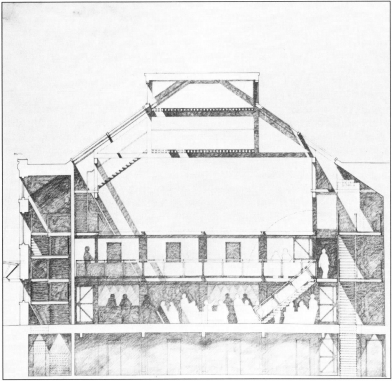

Architect's drawing of the Nia Centre, Manchester, to be housed in a converted Victorian theatre (drawing by Trevor Stratford for Mills Beaumont Leavey Architects)

An identified gap in provision of this sort can be regarded as a good reason for considering building.

INADEQUATE EXISTING FACILITIES
Establishing whether or not there is a need for a new building is less straightforward where provision for the arts already exists, but is considered to be inadequate or unsatisfactory.

Organisations can outgrow their buildings. Areas can change with the population drifting away or being replaced by people with different needs and aspirations. Interest in the arts can expand and where provision has been made at a fairly basic level, those who use it may press for better facilities.

In such situations as these, research is needed to establish the validity of the case for building. Alternative solutions should also be considered, for example:

- enabling an existing organisation to use its building more effectively. This might be achieved by upgrading existing accommodation, adapting the use of the building to changed circumstances, or establishing priorities in the use of the building and dis-

carding peripheral activities which take up a lot of time or space;

- making use of facilities owned by other organisations (e.g. using a school drama unit or a gymnasium). Often relatively small scale improvements can make a great difference for the arts use;

- establishing links with nearby arts facilities. Where the local community can only support the occasional event of a particular type or scale, linking with a neighbouring facility publicising it's events and organising booking and transport facilities may prove an acceptable solution, at least in the short term.

NEW OPPORTUNITIES
There are occasions where an opportunity presents itself. An interesting site or building becomes available or a new complex is planned, which could provide facilities for the arts. Any such opportunity needs to be carefully assessed in terms of what if offers the arts, whether it is suitable for the proposed use and how it is to be run and financed.

WHO IS GOING TO USE THE PROVISION?
Where new arts provision is being considered, some research is required to establish the potential audience or user groups. For a major new facility, a professional market research consultant may need to be brought in at this stage.

This question also needs to be asked when an arts company is planning to relocate to an adjacent area or alter its existing facilities.

USER GROUPS
An arts facility may be directed towards one particular group in the community or may aim to attract a range of ages and interests. If it is to be specialised provision, the target group needs to be identified before any user assessment is undertaken.

Arts Council Touring (Marketing and Information) has carried out a series of studies analysing user groups for arts events. The information is categorised in terms of region and art form.

CATCHMENT AREAS
The term 'catchment area' is used to describe the extent of the surrounding area from which support can be drawn. There are no firm rules on which to base the calculations, as a range of factors has to be taken into account. These include the availability of comparable facilities elsewhere in the area, the interests (and affluence) of the local community, the individuality, quality and scale of what is to be offered, the adequacy of public transport and the road network. For example, performances by the National Companies, whether in their London bases or on tour to the major regional centres, will draw audiences from 30 miles or more. Small rural centres may serve a population living within ten or even fifteen miles whereas a small urban

centre, particularly if it has a strong participatory programme, could have a catchment area of less than a mile.

EXISTING PROVISION
In order to provide a balance of facilities within an area, the initial study needs to look at what provision already exists, identifying the gaps and making an assessment of the range and quality of what is available.

The fact that there are other facilities in an area need not preclude new facilities being built, provided the potential for both can be established. The grouping of theatres in particular areas of London demonstrates that one space can generate support for another. In several cities, the success of one new arts building has led to others being provided in the same area.

EXISTING GROUPS AND ORGANISATIONS
Contact should be made with organisations and groups to establish the level, range and areas of interest. In any area there are groups of people interested in arts provision such as schools and colleges, youth groups, live music groups, dramatic or photographic societies, local craftspeople, choral societies and church choirs.

NEW AUDIENCES AND USER GROUPS
The level of interest should not be underestimated. Experience has shown that new buildings frequently attract a larger number of users than was anticipated and that, once a facility is open and operating successfully, the range of events in which any one group participates is extended.

WHAT FORM OF ARTS PROVISION IS REQUIRED?
In many situations, the proposed arts use is already determined before any detailed work begins. Most of those initiating a building project will have decided at the outset whether they want a performance space or an exhibition gallery, a major concert hall or an arts centre. This is not necessarily all there is to be considered. Increasingly, the main arts activity forms only the core of the arts use. Once this core activity is established (it will determine the nature of the spaces provided), opportunities for a wider range of compatible uses can be explored.

There is also a range of style of presentation and productions both within the individual art forms and within the various scales of arts facility. Art can be presented formally or informally: it can be designed for a space with a large volume or for a more intimate arrangement; it can be mainly traditional or can seek to explore new ways of expression. These different approaches need to be reflected in the design of the spaces which are to house them.

In some cases, the initial idea is to provide a space which will accommodate as wide a range of arts activities as possible. This cannot be achieved by building a large non-specific space and labelling it 'multi-purpose'. To provide adequate facilities for the arts, each of the proposed uses needs to be identified so that its specific requirements can be met. In practice, it is more cost effective and practical to limit the range of uses to a short-list of compatible forms.

The arts and the buildings which house them are continually evolving. It is worth spending some time, at this stage, not only looking at existing facilities but also talking to artists and people working in the arts about their current ideas, plans and projects. (Festivals provide good opportunities for seeing new work and meeting a range of people.) A new building is going to be a fixture for several decades. It has not only to respond to present needs but also to anticipate future developments.

(Additional information is given in Section 2 in the chapter on 'Arts and Venues' and Section 3 in the chapter on 'Multi-purpose and Shared Provision'.)

WHAT SORT OF BUILDING IS NEEDED?
The type of building provision which is made needs to relate to the use to which it is put. Given this general principle there are a number of possibilities which can be considered.

These include new purpose built, multi-use or shared use facilities, extending an existing arts building, or converting another building to arts use. The availability of suitable sites, the state of the existing building and the scope it offers for extension and improvement, the availability of suitable alternative buildings, the amount of money which can be raised, as well as the size and scope of the proposed project will all influence the final decision.

(The advantages and disadvantages of the various options are discussed in Section 2 in the chapter on 'Site and Buildings'.)

WHAT SIZE SHOULD IT BE?
The size of a facility is related to:
- the type of activity it is designed to house. Large scale works, whether in performance or exhibition, need large scale spaces. A full orchestra, for instance, needs a certain volume within the auditorium for it to be heard to its best effect. Many drama productions require more intimate spaces with a closer relationship between the performers and the audience;

- how many people are likely to use it. This is related to the density of the local population as well as to whether the facility is to be broadly based or more specialised;

- how much money is available to build and run it. While a large space may generate more income, it will also cost more to run. If the revenue funding which is likely to be available is insufficient to support a large facility, it is advisable to scale down the provision. On the other hand, many existing facilities are too small. A third of all arts centres, for example, have performance spaces seating fewer than 100 people. At this scale, the economics need to be carefully

studied as the amount of subsidy required,
relative to size, can be substantial.

IS THERE SCOPE FOR CO-OPERATION?

Many new arts buildings result from the co-
operative efforts of a number of organisations.
Links can be established between arts organisations and educational bodies to extend the range
and use of a proposed facility. Some sport and
arts mixes are compatible as are a mix of arts and
community activities. Some arts spaces can be
used for conferences, meetings, receptions or
leisure activities. Related commercial interests
(e.g. shops for music, books, dance equipment,
etc. and recording, photographic and video
facilities) can be provided with space in an arts
complex on terms which benefit both interests.
Studio space can mix with craft related light
industrial units.

Recent new developments demonstrate increasing scope for co-operation between arts groups
and development bodies - local authorities,
development corporations and commercial
developers. Semi-derelict sites have been redeveloped using the arts as a catalyst for drawing in
other interests and arts facilities have been
included in new commercially based developments to create a focus for a scheme. (See
Section 2 in the chapter on 'Planning Gain and
Development Opportunities'.)

HOW IS IT TO BE FINANCED?

The question of finance is crucial to the whole
process of planning, designing and building a
new facility. As money, or the lack of it, has an
effect on virtually every aspect of the project, an
assessment of costs needs to be made right at the
outset.

There are two elements to the cost of providing
facilities for the arts. The first is the capital cost
(i.e. the one-off cost of designing, constructing
and equipping the new building). The second is
the revenue cost (i.e. the continuing year-by-year
costs of running the facility). These costs are
inter-related and have to be worked out together.

(Information on capital costs and on revenue
costs is given in Section 2 in the chapters on
'Finance and Funding' and 'Arts and Venues'
respectively.)

WHO IS GOING TO MANAGE IT?

Some of the groups or organisations involved in
the planning and building of arts facilities may
not want to be responsible for running them once
they have been completed. For instance, a local
group may want to find a user for an attractive old
building it has acquired. Similarly a developer
may recognise the need for arts provision in a
newly built complex but may not want a continuing involvement in the project. In such cases, an
end user needs to be identified and some sort of
organisation set up before any detailed planning
work is undertaken. Where the end user is a
producing arts company, it is important that its
members are consulted at an early stage so that
their requirements can be set out in the brief.

(Section 2 gives information on the management
options in the chapter on 'Arts and Venues'.)

TESTING THE FEASIBILITY

Before the proposal is developed in any greater
detail, it is worth stepping back and spending
some time ensuring that it is both technically and
financially viable. This process is an important
one as it establishes the foundation on which the
project is based. As the project progresses
further, through the detailed planning, briefing,
design and building stages, the cost of rectifying
mistakes becomes increasingly expensive. Time
and money spent on testing the proposals should,
therefore, be seen as an investment which can
save resources in the long term.

The main areas to be considered are:
- the proposed uses
- the building and/or site
- the financial implications

These three elements are intrinsically linked.
(They are sometimes referred to as 'the planning
triangle'.) The range and scale of the proposed
uses determines the design and size of the
building. The design and size of the proposed
building has a direct affect on the capital and
running costs. The amount of money available to
build and run the arts facility places limitations on
both the building design and its proposed uses.
Any changes which are proposed in one of these
elements automatically affects the other two. This
means that the various elements have to be
assessed together. Where a number of specialists
are involved, they need to work as a co-ordinated
team.

THE PROPOSED USES

Testing this element involves checking:
- whether the demand for the activities or the
  facility exists or can be created;

- whether there is sufficient arts product
  available for the type of building proposed;
  (See the chapter in Section 2 on 'Arts and
  Venues.')

- whether the proposed uses are compatible in
  terms of times of use as well as space requirements.

THE BUILDING AND/OR SITE

Checks need to be carried out to ensure that the
site or building is suitable for the proposed uses
in terms of location, accessibility, planning
legislation, space requirements, etc. (See the
chapter in Section 2 on 'Site and Buildings'.)

If there is some doubt as to whether a site can
accommodate the amount of space required or
whether a building can be adapted to provide the
spaces needed, it may be necessary to appoint an
architect to prepare a 'block plan' or 'outline
design'.

THE FINANCIAL IMPLICATIONS

The cost implications should be analysed in some
detail at this stage.

Capital expenditure needs to be analysed in terms of cash flow as well as the total sums required.

With an existing building the estimates need to cover both the cost of making good the fabric and the cost of converting and fitting out the building for arts use.

Where financial resources are very limited, it is advisable to appoint the architect and quantity surveyor to undertake a feasibility study. If the estimated cost is well in excess of what can be raised, the project can be revised or phased or, at the worst, abandoned at this stage. Though the feasibility study will involve some expenditure, it will be very much less than the costs of designing a project which cannot be built. Design fees are payable whether or not the project proceeds to be built.

The revenue estimates need to look at the total cost package. The income will be derived from a number of sources: box office, entrance charges and related sales, commercial sales and lettings, catering, grants, sponsorships and donations. Expenditure is incurred in running and maintaining the building, providing an administration and paying for arts events.

(Further information on the subjects outlined above is given in Section 2.)

DEVELOPING THE DETAILED PROPOSAL
Before the brief can be drawn up, additional studies may be required to work out the patterns of use, the working relationships and the specialist requirements, as all these have an effect on the design of the building.

To establish the patterns of use, an outline programme needs to be drawn up to show the range of events planned to take place over a year together with a more detailed analysis based on a shorter period (e.g. one month).

A staffing chart is also needed showing the numbers and responsibilities of the staff required, the staff structures and how the areas of work need to relate to one another. Managerial and administrative staff, artists and performers, technical and support staff all have to be included.

Very specialised areas, such as the stage/ auditorium layout for a theatre or concert hall, are often developed in advance of the main structure, as they have an effect on the type of building to be provided. A theatre consultant or other specialist designer would undertake this work. The detailed specification would then form part of the brief.

Where a building is required to adapt to a range of uses, studies may need to be carried out at this stage to work out how the necessary flexibility is to be achieved.

If a number of organisations want to be involved in the design decisions (e.g. where two separate authorities are paying for the building or where the initiating body plans to lease the building to another organisation), it may be advisable to commission the architect to produce an outline scheme so that the general approach to the design can be agreed.

PREPARING THE BRIEF

The 'brief' is the technical term used to describe the set of instructions which the client gives to the architect. The architect's design is based on the client's brief. Proper briefing is, therefore, the key element to the success of a building project. If an architect is inadequately or incorrectly briefed, the designs he/she produces will reflect this, as will the end product - the building.

CONTENTS AND PRESENTATION
Architects receive briefs in widely differing forms. At one extreme, the architect is presented with a bulky document specifying every detail. This system tends to be used by large organisations involved in a number of fairly repetitive building projects where a standard brief merely has to be adapted to a particular site. The problem with a brief of this type is that it gives no opportunity for discussion or development and, at its worst, reproduces flawed solutions. It is not an appropriate form of briefing for arts buildings.

At the other extreme, the architect is asked to design a building for a particular purpose and given no detailed information. The design of the building is then developed through a series of discussions between the architect and the client. This system has occasionally been used by arts organisations and has produced some innovative projects. Its success depends very much on the dedication and skills of the individual architect and client, and the continuity between the two individuals is essential. It has too great an element of risk to be recommended as a briefing style for general use.

The style of brief which is recommended is one which starts with a written statement of the objectives and includes a detailed list of the requirements. This document forms the basis for the brief. It is then developed through discussions between the architect and client during which the architect is able to seek clarification of the client's requirements, explore alternative methods of approach and outline possible solutions. This dialogue is an important element in the design process.

The brief should start with a clear, simple statement setting out the objectives of the client organisation in commissioning a building project, the purpose the building is intended to serve and the scale of what is envisaged. This applies equally to a new building, a conversion or an improvement scheme.

The brief then defines and details the activities which the building is intended to house. If, for instance, the building is to provide a theatre space, the brief needs to consider what type of productions are to be shown. Scale is important, as is style of presentation. The work done during the feasibility and development stages (see chapter above on 'Drawing Up and Developing a Proposal') forms the basis for this part of the brief.

Having established what the main areas of activity are, the client then needs to look at the spaces which are required to house these activities. Spaces can be defined by function or by form. Defining by function means that the brief describes the purposes the space is intended to serve. For example, it might specify 'a dressing room, designed to provide changing and make-up facilities for four people who could be actors, opera singers or dancers etc.'. The alternative is to define by form, for example 'a room 17.4 square metres, with a working top along two walls extending 4.8m and projecting 450mm etc.'. For most arts buildings, the method of defining by function is preferable. This allows the architect more flexibility in the design. It also leaves the responsibility with the architect for ensuring that the spaces provided not only serve the purpose for which they are designed but also fulfil any related statutory requirements. There will, however, be some buildings when a detailed brief, specifying layout and dimensions, is appropriate. These would, in the main, relate to specialised arts spaces where the client has a very clear idea of what form the space is to take, or where a specialist consultant has been employed to design a particular area. In other situations, if dimensions are given, it is generally more useful if they give guidance on the minimum acceptable standards rather than setting out exact specifications.

The brief needs to be both specific (in that it identifies all the requirements) and flexible (in that it leaves the architect sufficient scope to create a building which is more than a mere collection of spaces). The way a brief is worded is important. In general it is preferable to use words such as 'suggest', 'recommend', and 'it is desirable that ...', which leave the architect scope to offer an alternative solution rather than terms such as 'must' and 'it is obligatory that ..'. The latter terms need only be used where the requirements outlined constitute the only acceptable way of achieving the given objective. The brief also needs to give an indication of the financial parameters of the project. Some clients will have sufficient experience of building to feel confident in setting a target figure. At this early stage, however, many organisations will have very little idea of what a building will cost. In this case, the brief can only set the context (i.e. explaining how the project is to be financed, making comparisons with other arts projects, etc.).

Where financial resources are very limited, studies to establish estimated costs should be undertaken at the feasibility stage.

PRODUCING A BRIEF
While a good brief will draw on ideas and recommendations from many different sources, the work of putting it together is best undertaken by one person.

Brief writing is a demanding job, as the brief, in effect, constitutes the 'verbal plan' of the building. It cannot be rushed and needs to be carried out by someone with sufficient authority to question and argue with people at every level in the organisation.

The person delegated to write the brief could be the project co-ordinator, the potential administrator or the director of the existing organisation. Where large, specialised facilities are being considered, consultants could be brought in.

EXISTING ORGANISATIONS
Where the building is to be designed to house an existing organisation, a careful study needs to be made as to how the organisation functions, and decisions made as to whether it wishes to continue operating in the same way or whether it proposes to make changes once a new building is provided.

Individuals, and related groups within the existing organisation need to define what they do, the spaces they need to do it in, the facilities which they require and how they relate to other individuals and groups and to particular areas of a building (e.g. access to the exterior, ground floor position, etc.).

The person responsible for drawing up the brief then needs to collect this information together and identify overlapping areas of interest and potential points of conflict, establish priorities and work out what spaces can be shared. Where points of conflict cannot be satisfactorily resolved, this needs to be spelt out in the brief. This process may well be time consuming and involve a series of consultations with members of the organisation, both individually and as a group. Once the overall requirements are established, the writing of the brief is a meticulous process of listing, explaining, describing, detailing and pinpointing areas of specific need so that the architect knows what spaces are to be provided, what facilities are required, what relationships are important and what the overall feel of the building should be.

NEW FACILITIES
Whereas those working in an existing organisation will know what they want to do in a building and have a fairly clear idea of what spaces and facilities are required, with a new facility this has to be worked out before a brief can be drawn up. The initial processes of research and assessment should have established what is needed, and how it is to be provided. The nature, number, size and style of the spaces required and how these are to be fitted out can only be established once a proposal for the use of the building has been drawn up and costed. (See page 16.)

EXISTING BUILDINGS
With a new building the use dictates the form. With an existing building, especially one of historic or architectural interest, the form has to influence the use to which the building as a whole and its individual elements are put. The skill in converting an existing building to a new

use lies in the designer's ability to match spaces and activities. To help achieve this, the brief needs to set out aims and offer options rather than list a set of specific requirements. The best solutions tend to be developed more through discussions, in which ideas are considered, accepted, amended or rejected, until an outline scheme can be agreed.

CHECKLIST

The purpose of a brief is to describe and detail an individual building so that it can be designed to suit a specific set of requirements. The checklist which follows outlines the range of information which is likely to be needed.

The elements which make up a brief include:

ARTISTIC POLICY
Setting out the objectives of the initiating organi- sation, defining what the building is for, whom it will serve and how it will operate.

DESCRIPTION
Outlining the size, range and scope of the build- ing. Indicating what sort of building is required, the feel of the building and the way it is intended that the users will respond to it. How it relates to the local area, to its more immediate neighbours (the streetscape or surrounding environment) and to the site.

GENERAL REQUIREMENTS
Standard and quality. Types of finishes. Space standards. Quality of fittings. Design qualities (e.g. economic, robust, comfortable).

COST PARAMETERS
An indication of the overall budget with the maximum figure stated where this is important.

DEFINING THE USES
A detailed description of the uses to which the building is to be put. Consideration needs to be given at this stage to the full range of activities which the building is to accommodate. This includes any secondary uses - for example occasional activities, use of the spaces by outside organisations, etc. - as well as the necessary sup- porting activities (e.g. catering). Where a range of primary uses is proposed, priorities may have to be established.

DETAILING THE SPACES
A description of the main spaces required (and the necessary support areas) with information as to the purposes they serve and the ways in which they are to be used.

RELATIONSHIPS
The way the spaces relate one to another is important when the building is being used. Link- ages need to be set out and identified as 'essen- tial' or 'desirable'. Such links could be required between areas with related uses or between members of staff and areas of activity. The position of certain spaces in the building can be important (e.g. 'with direct exterior access' or 'ground floor level only').

THE SITE AND SURROUNDING AREA
The uses to which the spaces around the building are to be put need to be considered. These include access and unloading areas, parking for staff, for users and for people with disabilities, landscaping, screening, and external storage.

SPECIAL REQUIREMENTS
Information on particular aspects of the design such as:

- Shape, format or layout

- Level of services (heating and ventilation and humidity controls)

- Lighting requirements (where natural light is required this should be specified)

- Sound requirements (levels of insulation, acoustic standards, special equipment)

- Fitting out requirements (fixtures which need to be designed and built into the structure)

- Specifics (such as need for secure areas, disposal of waste, storage of flammable materials)

Section 3, 'Design Requirements' gives further information on the subjects outlined above.

THE DESIGN PROCESS

The design process begins with a detailed consid- eration of the brief. The architect and design con- sultants go through the brief with the initiating organisation. This organisation is referred to as 'the client' or 'the client body', as that is its relationship with the design team.

Once the requirements have been clarified, work can begin on the initial design. This needs to be approved by the client before detailed design work is put in hand. The designs are developed in detail and final approval is then sought. Instruc- tions are prepared for the building of the project and building contractors are invited to put in bids for the work. At this stage the design process is complete and the building process begins.

THE DESIGN TEAM
Architects are the only professional group trained and qualified in the design of buildings though other consultants are often brought in to work on specialist areas. For a small project, the architect may undertake the work on an individual basis, taking specialist advice only when he/she considers it necessary. In larger, or more special- ised schemes, a team of consultants is normally appointed to work together on the design of the building.

The design team can include:
Specialist Arts Designers - Theatre Consultants, Exhibition Designers, Acousticians;

Other design consultants - Interior Designers, Landscape Architects;

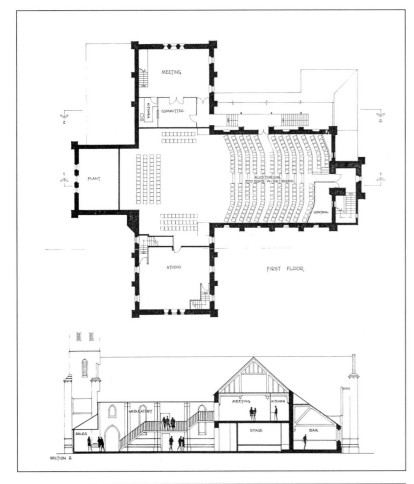

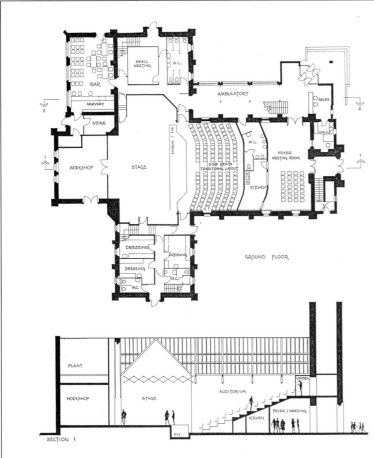

Engineers - Structural, Mechanical, Electrical;

Quantity and Building Surveyors.

It is important that the members of the design team are appointed on the basis of their compatibility as well as their individual expertise. The first member of the team to be appointed will normally make recommendations regarding the appointment of other consultants. In most cases, this will be the architect.

There are some multi-disciplinary design firms which are able to provide a range of expertise but it is unlikely that any one firm would be able to provide the full range of specialist advice required for a large scale arts project.

DESIGN TEAM FEES

Fees are negotiated individually with the various members of the design team. Where a number of specialist consultants are appointed, the main consultants may be prepared to adjust their fees accordingly.

As all fees are now negotiable and include a large number of variables, it is only possible to give indicative figures. In estimating the total costs of the design team, an allocation of 15% -20% of the building costs should be allowed. This figure probably needs to be increased to 20% -25% for work on existing buildings.

Most of the design fees are incurred before any building work starts. Information on the individual fee scales is available from the relevant professional institutes.

(See the chapter in Section 2 on 'Working with Consultants.')

THE CLIENT'S ROLE

It is important that the client continues to be closely involved with the project throughout the design stage to ensure that it is developed in accordance with his/her requirements. He/she needs to work with the team in defining what is needed, making decisions about what is to be provided and giving the necessary approvals to enable the work to proceed.

The design process is divided into a number of stages. These are outlined in the following text. At the end of each stage, the proposals have to be approved by the client before any further work is done. Once approval is given it has to be regarded as binding. For this reason, it is important that the client understands what is being proposed as the project progresses, what the cost implications are and what the plans mean in building terms.

Many people have difficulty in reading plans and are unable to visualise three dimensional spaces from drawings. If the client experiences problems in these areas it is up to him/her to ask the

Plans and sections showing Trinity Church, Gainsborough, converted to arts centre use
(drawings by Tom Benson architect)

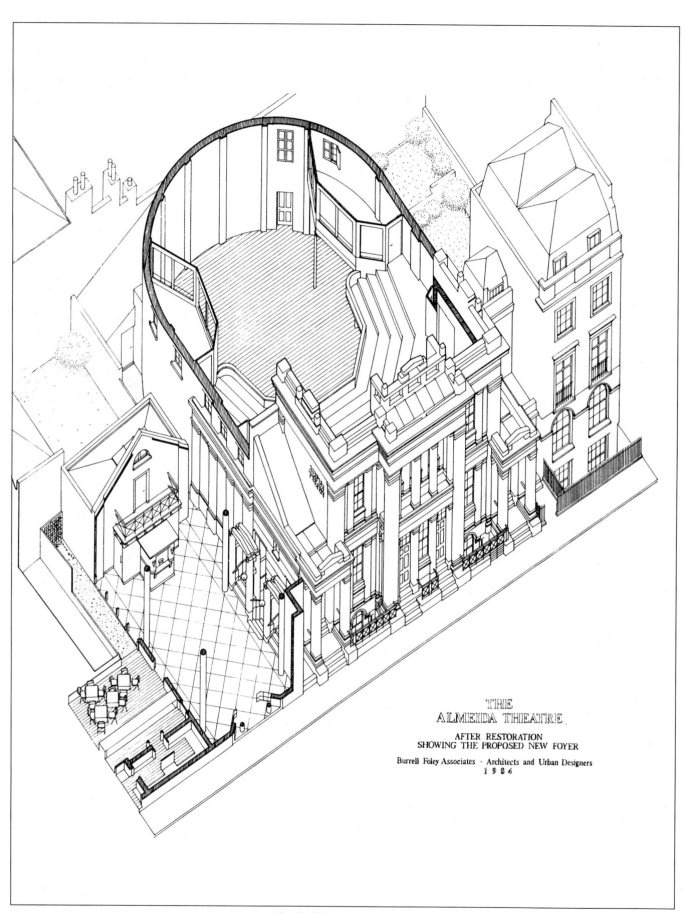

THE
ALMEIDA THEATRE
AFTER RESTORATION
SHOWING THE PROPOSED NEW FOYER

Burrell Foley Associates · Architects and Urban Designers
1 9 8 6

Almeida Theatre, Islington
Cutaway axonometric drawing of the converted building
(drawing by Burrell Foley Associates, Architects and Urban Designers)

Model of the new West Yorkshire Playhouse used for publicity and fundraising

architect to explain the proposals in more easily comprehended ways - for example, by relating a planned space to an existing space or by taking the client through a particular activity and tracing out the route on the plans.

PLANS AND DRAWINGS
The design team prepares a range of types of drawings in the course of designing a building. The following text gives a brief description of the information provided on the different drawings.

PLANS
Plans show the layout on a two dimensional basis. Location plans show the building in relation to the surrounding area (access routes, adjacent buildings), site plans show the position of the building on the site (they may include services, waste and water), floor plans show the layout and size of the spaces on each floor level. Roof plans may also be included. The position of doorways and windows is normally indicated on the floor plans, and changes in level are marked. Stairs are normally shown as divided between one floor and the next. Raked seating may also be illustrated in this way.

When the design is being developed in detail, plans are drawn up to show wiring, plumbing, ventilation, etc. as appropriate.

It is normal practice to include a compass mark on all plans. Where it is not identified the arrow points north.

SECTIONS
Sections represent a two dimensional slice of the building. They show heights and changes in level. Each section drawing should be identified - often letters such as 'AA' or 'BB' are used. This relates to the plans which are marked with points 'A' and 'A', 'B' and 'B', etc. which give the line (when joined) which the section follows.

ELEVATIONS
Elevations show the building facades (e.g. front elevation, side elevation, etc.). These give an indication of what the building will look like when a straight on view is taken from any particular side. They show the overall massing of the building, the shape of the roof, the position of windows and doorways and external detailing.

In reality, few buildings are seen from this straight on position, unless they are in an open position with a long vista. Seen from the street, much of the upper level will be masked by other parts of the building.

AXONOMETRICS
Axonometric drawings are three dimensional plans. They tend to be used for more specialist areas of presentation. They are useful for illustrating auditoria designs where the many changes of levels (raked seating, tiers, stage rises, etc.) are difficult to show with plans and sections.

PERSPECTIVE DRAWINGS
Perspective drawings are used to give an indication of what the completed building will look like. They are non-technical representations which can be used for clients' presentations and promotional purposes. A simple perspective drawing might be commissioned for use in a fundraising brochure. Where perspectives form part of a set of drawings, the position from which the building is shown should be marked on the plan (a directional arrow is normally used).

MODELS
Models can help get across a three-dimensional view of the proposed scheme. Simple block models are often used to explain and develop specialised areas, such as the auditorium. Models of the completed building can be useful for promotional purposes, but detailed models are expensive to produce.

All drawings, other than the perspective drawings, are produced to scale. The scale is shown on the drawing. Metric measurements are now standard.

DESIGN STAGES
The process of designing a building follows a number of recognised stages. All members of the design team work on a similar basis. The following summary is based on the definitions drawn up by The Royal Institute of British Architects (RIBA) and uses the RIBA terms.

PRELIMINARY SERVICES
While the proposal is being developed and the brief drawn up, the architect may be asked to advise on the overall scope of the building work, work out a general timetable, state what other design consultants will be needed and give a very broad indication of the cost.

More detailed design work could be required at this stage, for instance, to establish a cost estimate or work out whether a building could fit onto a difficult site.

Any work done at this stage is charged on a time basis.

THE INITIAL DESIGN: PHASE I
The design of a building starts when the architect

takes the client's brief. This is normally presented in the form of a written document setting out the client's requirements (see page 18). The architect and design consultants study the brief and come back to the client with a series of questions in order to clarify the instructions and establish the approach to the problem. This is an important process which aims to ensure that the design team is fully appraised of the client's intentions. Once the brief is established, the architect prepares outline designs. These set out the team's ideas on how the building will be designed, the use of the site or existing building, and the general layout showing how spaces relate to one another. It should also give an indication of what the building might look like and how much it could cost.

These outline proposals are presented to the client for approval. It is important that the client is satisfied that he/she has enough information to make an initial assessment and is confident that he/she understands what is proposed. Where there is doubt, the client should ask for more explanation and information. If the design approach is not acceptable, the client can ask for changes to be made. If it appears to be too expensive, then alternative solutions can be sought or the brief amended. (Costs estimates tend to increase as more detailed information is provided, so if the scheme appears to be too expensive at this stage it is advisable to amend the design and/or brief rather than take an optimistic risk.) When the client is satisfied that the basic approach is acceptable, that the outline design meets the requirements set out in the brief and that the initial cost estimate is in line with the overall budget, approval can be given for the design team to proceed with the design development.

THE INITIAL DESIGN: PHASE II
Once the general approach has been agreed the architect and other consultants work on the design, bringing in any amendments required by the client, and developing it to a stage which shows the scheme in sufficient detail for the client to agree the spatial arrangements, materials and appearance. At this stage, the architect should be able to provide the client with information on possible start and completion dates for the building project, and make application for detailed planning permission. Once again, the architect comes back to the client to explain the scheme, identifying any changes made and outlining the effect of such changes on the estimated cost and building programme. Once again, it is the responsibility of the client to make sure that everything is satisfactory before giving approval to proceed with the next stage.

While the assessment, approval and amendment of the design proposals have to be part of a continuing process, there are important break points in this process when decisions to proceed carry with them major cost implications. This is one such point. Up to this stage, the architect and consultants have been developing the design for the client's approval. Beyond this stage, the design work leads on to the construction of the building. If the commitment to proceed with the building cannot be made without reservation, there is no point in spending additional money on design fees. It is better to put the whole thing on ice until the problems are sorted out. It is obviously preferable to avoid having to reach such a decision at this late stage in the design as considerable fees will already have been incurred. Phases I and II together account for 35% of the architect's total fee.

THE DETAILED DESIGN
The design continues to be developed in greater detail. At this stage the client's approval is sought regarding the type of construction, the quality of the materials to be used and the standard of workmanship required. The architect co-ordinates the work being done by consultants, specialist contractors, sub-contractors and suppliers and obtains detailed information and quotations in connection with their work. At this stage, for instance, the mechanical engineers design the ventilation systems and the theatre consultant details fittings and equipment for the stage and auditorium.

It is important that the client remains closely involved with the project, as much of the arts related design work (e.g. seating, lighting, finishes) is worked out at this stage.

There are a number of regulations which govern the design and construction of buildings. They relate, in the main, to the safety of the construction and of the building in operation. The design is sufficiently advanced at this stage for approvals to be sought under the building acts, regulations and statutory requirements. It is the architect's job to make and negotiate such applications.

By the end of this stage, the client has a fully worked out scheme with the necessary approvals. It is possible to make a reasonably accurate estimate of the cost, though formal bills of quantities are not prepared until the next stage. (The bills of quantities are detailed lists of the materials which are required to construct the building. These lists are prepared by a Quantity Surveyor.)

GETTING READY TO GO TO TENDER
This phase of the design process is concerned with producing a set of requirements on which a building contractor can base his tender for the work. In addition to more detailed plans, the architect draws up a specification of requirements. The specification describes the materials which are to be used and the standards of construction. Much of the text of any building specification is standard - in line with the documents produced by the National Building Specification Service. Where it relates to one-off arts provision a detailed, individual specification is drawn up by the design team.

At the same time bills of quantities are prepared which list the nature, quality and amount of the building materials required.

All these documents have to be prepared in

sufficient detail to enable a contractor to prepare
a tender.

INVITING TENDERS

The architect, in consultation with the client,
draws up a list of building contractors which he/
she considers are capable of carrying out the
work. A shortlist of between four and eight firms
is normal, depending on the size and complexity
of the job. Some organisations have a statutory
obligation to accept the lowest tender submitted.
Where this is the case, care should be taken to
ensure that all the building contractors included
on the list are capable of carrying out the work to
a good standard and are financially sound.

The documents are sent to the contractors with
an invitation to tender for the work. The tender
sets out the basis on which the contractor is
prepared to carry out the building work and gives
a price for the job. This does not necessarily
represent the final cost of the work (see below
'The Building Contract').

Once the tenders are in, it is the architect's job to
appraise them, interpret them to the client and
advise on which one should be accepted. Further
negotiations may be required before a final
decision can be reached.

The nature of the building industry is such that it
is possible to receive a set of tenders which are
all substantially in excess of the estimates
prepared by the design team. This is not necessarily a reflection on the competence of that team.
Prices fluctuate with supply and demand, not only
within the labour force but with building materials in an international market. Where tenders are
received sufficiently over the budget to threaten
the viability of a project, it may be advisable to
postpone the construction until the market
settles. The alternative is to make substantial cuts
in the scheme. Where possible, it is preferable to
phase the scheme or reduce the scope of the
facilities rather than cut back on standards of
quality.

There is an increasing trend not to go out to
tender, but to obtain a negotiated management
contract from one selected contractor who will
co-ordinate the work of other specialist suppliers
and sub-contractors. This may be appropriate for
large contracts or contracts where time is of the
essence (e.g. commercial developments seeking
an early return on the capital invested). It is
unlikely to be the most suitable method for arts
organisations where speed of completion is less
important than the overall cost of the construction work.

The tender stage marks the end of the design
process.

DESIGN/BUILD SYSTEMS

Some building work is carried out on a design-
build basis, sometimes referred to as a 'package
deal'. The client (the organisation or individual
requiring a building) draws up the brief and
invites bids to be submitted, accompanied by
design proposals. The contractors and developers
then work with their in-house architectural team
or commission independent architects to draw up
outline proposals. These are costed and on this
basis, the contractor or developer works out his
price for the job.

This system is used quite frequently, and with
some success, for commercial developments. It
would not generally be considered to be the best
way of designing arts buildings as these are one-
off buildings which depend on a carefully developed brief and an experienced designer or design
team for their success.

THE BUILDING PROCESS

This chapter looks at the building process when
the work is undertaken by a building contractor.
This is the recommended procedure for all but
very small scale improvement schemes.

Building is a complex process which inevitably
involves a number of unknown factors and few
building projects reach completion without some
problems. Careful planning can help to minimise
the problems and a competent design team will
also have the experience to deal with those which
do occur.

THE BUILDING CONTRACT

As soon as the building contractor has been
selected and the price agreed, a contract can be
prepared. This is normally based on one of the
standard formats which are drawn up and regularly revised by a body made up of representa-
tives of the various interested parties within the
building industry (the Joint Contracts Tribunal).
It is the architect's job to explain the contract to
the client.

The contract is made with one main contractor
who is responsible for the whole of the construction work. It may include fitting out and furnishing or may terminate once the building shell is
complete, with the fitting out and furnishing
being undertaken under a separate contract. In
many projects, a number of sub-contractors are
employed to deal with specialist areas. It is the
responsibility of the main contractor to plan the
building programme and ensure that the various
sub-contractors know when their input is scheduled.

While the builder works out the programe and
gets ready to start, it is the client's responsibility,
with the advice of the architect, to ensure that the
site is ready. Insurance needs to be arranged at
this stage. The building programme gives a
completion date for the construction work. This
date forms part of the agreement between the
client and the contractor. (In this context, the
correct title for the client of the architect is
'building owner', and once the contractor is
signed the building owner becomes the 'em-
ployer' of the contractor, and that is the title used
in the contract.)

CLAIMS AND ADDITIONAL WORK

The contractor's tender gives a price for the
construction work. The figure could relate to a

fixed price contract or to a fluctuating price contract. In a fluctuating price contract, changes in the cost of building materials are reflected in the construction costs. Most contracts are negotiated on a fixed price basis but the agreement is only valid for a given period. If the building work continues beyond a given date the contract may go on to a fluctuating price basis.

A fixed price contract does not necessarily mean that the final account (the cost of the construction work when the job has been completed) will be the same figure as that set out in the tender documents. In some cases, the end figure can be substantially in excess of that envisaged. There are a number of 'claims' which can be made by the contractor. A 'claim' is an additional amount of money which is payable by the building owner to the contractor based on loss of profit and additional expense. The most usual bases on which a claim is made are delays and unforeseen additional work.

There are three types of delay which can affect the progress of the building project.

Firstly, there could be delays in the building programme for which the contractor is responsible (e.g. insufficient men on the job, bad organisation of work schedule), which result in the building not being ready by the agreed completion date. In such cases, the owner may be able to make a claim against the building contractor.

Secondly, there are delays which occur through circumstances outside the control of either the owner or the contractor (e.g. earthquakes, very bad weather, dock strikes). In such cases, no claims can be made by either party.

Thirdly, delays may be caused by the owner, the owner appointed sub-contractors, or the owner's consultants. This is a complicated area which has given rise to a great deal of study and a certain amount of litigation over the last decade. The most likely cause of delay in this area is where a sub-contractor is unable to meet the agreed work schedule and so puts back the whole building programme. For example, at a given stage in the building work, the ventilation system needs to be installed. If the equipment is not available, the work on the building has to stop. The cost of keeping workers on site during this period is additional to that given in the contract. Where the owner (or the owner's consultants) nominates the sub-contractor (i.e. states which one should be appointed), the owner is responsible for any delays which the sub-contractor may cause. Where the contractor nominates the sub-contractor, he is responsible for any such delays. Obviously, it would appear to be in the client's interest to avoid nominating sub-contractors but with arts buildings, where the equipment needs to be very carefully selected and there is a limited range of specialist suppliers, this is not always desirable.

The other main reason for claims being made by the contractor is unforeseen additional work. Even with competent preparations and planning on the part of the design team, it is not always possible to avoid additional work having to be done by the contractor. With a new building, most of the problems which occur relate to the underground conditions and how these affect the foundations. It is normal practice to test the site conditions - a number of bore holes are made but these cannot cover the whole site. Once work starts on digging out for the foundations, all sorts of things can be discovered - old wells, underground streams, forgotten sewerage systems, areas of soft ground, or even the Rose Theatre. With an existing building, there is much greater scope for discovering unforeseen problems. For instance, the poor state of the timber or brickwork may only be apparent when plaster is stripped away.

The client also has to meet the cost of additional work resulting from changes to the specification. Such changes should be avoided once the contract has been let but there will be occasions when circumstances require them. For instance, a building failure might occur on a completely different building project which draws attention to problems relating to the use of some building material, structural detail or piece of equipment already specified, which were not previously known.

While it is not possible to avoid all possible claims, experienced consultants are aware of the potential problems and have developed techniques in negotiating the building contract which help to minimise the claims potential. Where a large or complex building is planned, it is advisable to appoint architects and design consultants with experience of designing and administering similar schemes. (See the chapter in Section 2 on 'Working with Consultants'.)

More information on construction costs is given in Section 2 in the chapter on 'Finance and Funding'.

THE CONSTRUCTION PERIOD
SITE SUPERVISION

The contract is an agreement between the building owner and the building contractor. It is the contractor's responsibility to ensure that the work is carried out in accordance with the contract (of which the architect's instructions form a part). The architect looks after the owner's interests and makes sure that the contract is fairly administered. The architect is expected to visit the site to check on progress but is not responsible for the day to day supervision of the building work.

In large scale projects it is usual practice to appoint a Clerk of Works to inspect the building work, either on a full or part-time basis depending on the nature of the job and the terms of his appointment. The Clerk of Works is appointed by the building owner, on the advice of the architect, and he looks after the owner's interest while the contractor is on site. Clerks of Works are skilled building operatives (they will often have worked previously as general foremen) and will normally be members of the Institute of Clerks of Work.

For smaller projects, the building owner should consider appointing a surveyor to check that the work is being carried out in accordance with the specification.

THE BUILDING TEAM

The rest of the on site building team is employed by the contractor who is also responsible for co-ordinating the work of the sub-contractors. The construction work is supervised by the General Foreman who is the leader of the building team and responsible for the site and work. Depending on the size of the project, he is supported by a number of individual trade foremen, each with their own team of tradesmen. The trades in the building industry cover areas of skilled work such as bricklaying, plastering, carpentry, plumbing, painting, glazing, etc. They are supported by other specialised groups concentrating on such things as concrete work, flooring, etc. Some groups of workers move from one site to another as their skills are needed, others work on one project throughout its duration. The general foreman remains with the project.

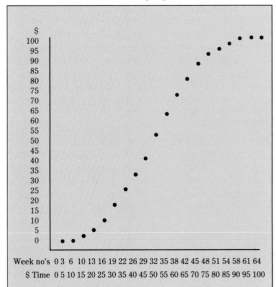

Example of 'S' CURVE showing money spent relating to time elapsed

Week no's	0 3 6 10 13 16 19 22 26 29 32 35 38 42 45 48 51 54 58 61 64
$ Time	0 5 10 15 20 25 30 35 40 45 50 55 60 65 70 75 80 85 90 95 100

In small building firms, the trade work is normally sub-contracted. This practice is becoming increasingly common in larger scale organisations. Where this is the case, it is important that the quality of work is carefully controlled.

ACCESS TO THE BUILDING SITE

Once the main contractor moves onto the site, it becomes his responsibility. Access to the building site is controlled in the interests of security and safety and any visitors have to report to the general foreman before entering the site. This applies to the client and members of his/her organisation as well as to more general visitors.

Where improvements are being made to an existing building, normal activities can only continue if the areas where the building work is taking place can be sealed off from the rest of the space and provided with separate access.

LENGTH OF CONTRACT

The length of time for which the building contract runs, depends on the size and complexity of the

project and the nature of the agreement with the contractor. The contract period for a medium sized project (e.g. a single arts building such as a theatre or arts centre) is likely to be in the region of 12 to 24 months.

There is a system of building known as 'fast track' but the cost premium for speed is a heavy one. The additional expense is unlikely to be justified in an arts project.

STAGE PAYMENTS

During the construction period, the owner has to ensure that payments are made to the building contractor as and when they become due. At pre-determined stages (e.g. every two months) the architect certifies the amount due to the builder based on how much work has been completed on site. The amounts vary according to the work done (in some work stages a great deal of expenditure is incurred in a very short time, in others it is more evenly spread over a longer period). The expenditure in a building project tends to follow a pattern (the 'S' curve illustrated here) so it is possible to estimate stage payments in advance.

POTENTIAL PROBLEMS

It is likely that some problems will occur during the progress of any building project. Many of these require decisions from the building's owner - advised by the architect and the consultants - to resolve them. It is important, then, that someone within the owner organisation is given overall responsibility during this period and has the necessary authority to make a quick response. For example, it could happen that certain components vital to the progress of the work are unobtainable. In such a case, the client needs to agree alternatives or accept responsibility for the delay.

The most difficult situation to deal with is where the owner runs out of money or is unable to meet a stage payment when it becomes due. The contractor can then withdraw his team from the site and only continue working if compensation is made for delays. To avoid this happening, arrangements need to be made to cover the building costs well in advance of the contract being let.

Another major problem is where the contractor goes into liquidation during the course of the contract. (The liquidation rate in the construction industry tends to be higher than the average.) If this happens the client faces long delays while the crisis is coming to a head and then in getting the contractor off the site and going out to tender again. Subsequent tenders are likely to be substantially more expensive. There can be no guarantees that any contractor will remain solvent, but the chances can be increased by selecting firms with a background of sound financial controls rather than those with a reputation for doing things more cheaply. Tenders which come in well below the market rate need to be regarded with caution.

It is possible for accidents to occur while the building work is in progress. (For example, part of the building or an adjacent building could collapse, or the site be flooded.) Such accidents may result from negligence on the part of some member of either the design team or the building team. The building owner should ensure that the consultants and the contractor are adequately insured. For this reason, it is inadvisable to accept technical services offered on an informal basis, even where they are provided free and relate to a small project. It may also be worth considering taking out insurance to cover the costs of litigation on the part of the owner.

COMPLETION AND HANDOVER

On completion, the architect is responsible for explaining the building to the client (i.e. making sure he/she knows where everything is located and how it works). There is an agreed period in the building contract when any defects discovered have to be put right. (Defects which occur after that date have to be settled by negotiation.) At the end of this period the final account is settled. The final account comprises the sum of money stated in the contract plus any additional costs, less any savings that have been made. The additional costs are agreed between the architect, quantity surveyor and contractor. They comprise, in the main, compensation for delays incurred by the client, his/her consultants and nominated sub-contractors and payment for additional work. As these claims are subject to interpretation and negotiation (and occasionally litigation), the final account may only be settled some time after the building work has been completed.

PUBLIC RELATIONS OPPORTUNITIES

There are various stages of achievement which are marked in the building programme and can serve as the basis for useful publicity to help a fundraising campaign or retain public interest. The first of these is when the contractor moves onto the site. (This used to be illustrated with pictures of a local dignatory 'cutting the first sod'.) The second is the 'topping out ceremony' which marks the completion of the structure of the building. (Traditionally it was celebrated with rounds of beer for all the workmen when the roof went onto a building.) The final stage is the 'handover ceremony' when the building is formally checked out and handed over by the contractor to the client.

THE BUILDING IN USE

When the building work is completed, the architect has to explain to the owner how everything works, give guidance on maintenance and provide drawings showing the main building lines and the position of services. At the time the building is handed over, it should be in pristine condition with everything in working order.

LIFE CYCLE PLANNING

As soon as a building is opened for use, it starts to deteriorate. The different elements of the building all have a given life span - some require to be repaired or replaced very frequently, others last for many years but none last indefinitely. Because it takes a while for buildings to show an overall deterioration people tend to disregard the fact that a new building is a depreciating asset. This view is encouraged by the way buildings appear to appreciate in value. The appreciation in value, in fact, relates to the value of the land which the building occupies and the increased cost of replacement or of alternative accommodation. In maintenance terms, each bit of the new building can be regarded in the same way as a car: an asset which depreciates in value until it needs to be replaced. In accounting terms, the cost of a new car is charged over a given number of years and then an increased amount is put into the budget to cover the cost of a replacement. If a building is seen as the sum of its parts, it can be regarded in the same way. However, this is not common accounting practice and the timescale over which the whole building deteriorates tends to make this approach impracticable.

Maintaining a building over its lifetime requires regular and planned expenditure to be incurred. Few arts buildings in this country have adequate sums set aside for maintenance and renewal. Many are allowed to deteriorate gradually until they are forced to close down or launch an appeal for a major refurbishment project. Neglecting a building over a period of many years means that a valuable and costly asset is being used inefficiently. During the time when it is becoming rundown, it will be expensive to run, will suffer a fall-off in use and will no longer be able to attract good quality arts events. The refurbishment will be costly, time-consuming and may well close the facility down for a long period.

Maintenance and renewals are best carried out on a programmed basis. The alternative is to wait until something goes wrong. This more pragmatic approach can seem attractive in that money is only spent when it is obviously necessary to do so, but there are a number of inherent problems. Costs cannot be regulated or budgeted for in advance. Unplanned work can create additional work or negate work that has just been carried out. It is also more expensive to bring in a series of different building firms, all on short or emergency contracts, to tackle one problem after another, than it is to employ a single contractor on a regular basis.

A set amount (calculated as a percentage of the building replacement cost and updated regularly to take account of inflation) needs to be allocated on an annual basis and set aside for maintenance and renewal. Major works such as rewiring, repointing brickwork, replacement of roofing materials, etc. occur infrequently so part of the maintenance budget should go into a fund to allow for one-off heavy expenditure.

Areas should be programmed for redecoration according to a worked out schedule. (Not all areas will require redecoration on the same basis - some may need to be repainted annually whilst others may last over ten years.)

MAINTENANCE

The regular maintenance of a building helps to keep it in a good state of repair and to reduce replacement costs in the longer term.

Scaffolding erected in the auditorium at the Trinity Arts
Centre to install a radiant heat gas- fire and central
heating system and to paint the ceiling
(photograph by David Markson)

The routine areas to be covered include:

- cleaning. Regular major cleaning sessions need to be scheduled in addition to the day-to-day cleaning;

- servicing. Regular servicing needs to be carried out on all installations. These include the heating and ventilation systems, lifts, security systems, as well as the technical equipment related to the arts use;

- replacement of damaged fittings and equipment. Arts buildings get heavy use. Many of the users are unfamiliar with the buildings and with how the fixtures operate so things get broken. Regular (i.e. weekly) maintenance checks mean that breakages, loose fittings, tears in fabrics, etc. can be spotted and fixed at an early stage.

The equipment also needs to be maintained (e.g. stage and bleacher units).

It is advisable to keep a stock of spare parts and matching fittings or make sure that they are readily available when needed.

RESPONSIBILITY FOR MAINTENANCE

In all organisations, someone should be given the responsibility for planning and overseeing the maintenance of the building: the cleaning, renewals, replacements and larger scale works. This is an administrative job and requires an understanding of how the building works and an appreciation of its quality. This person should be responsible for establishing standards of cleaning and maintenance and for training staff in the use of the building, fittings and equipment.

He/she needs to have available the information which the architect handed over at the completion of the building, keep records of any work carried out subsequently, have a file of instructions on the use of equipment and fittings and keep notes on where replacement stock can be obtained.

2 SPECIFICS

The planning, design and construction of an arts building can be seen as a logical series of steps which takes the initiating organisation through a process starting with the initial idea and continuing until the building is open and operating. This process is outlined in Section 1.

During this process, information needs to be collected, advice sought and a number of practical measures taken.

All arts projects are different. They start from different points, they have different objectives and so they need to follow different routes. While most organisations need advice and information to help them through the process outlined in Section I, they do not all need the same advice and information. They need guidance which is specific to their particular project.

For this reason, the 'specifics' (the areas of more detailed information) have been separated from the 'process' and they are set out in this section. It is not intended to be read consecutively (though an initial quick reading may help to give an overview of what is involved in an arts building project), but to be referred to, as needed, throughout the early stages of the planning and design process.

The information is grouped under three main headings:
- Arts and Venues
- Sites and Buildings
- Finance and Funding

with additional information under two further headings:
- Planning Gain and Development Opportunities (which relates to both 'Finance and Funding' and 'Sites and Buildings')

- Working with Consultants (which relates to all three)

This section does not cover the design of arts spaces. This is discussed in Section 3, 'Design Requirements'.

ARTS AND ARTS VENUES

This chapter covers a range of topics relating to the organisation, planning and management of the buildings which house the arts. The information is divided into three parts:

SPACES FOR THE ARTS
which looks at the main categories of arts buildings and the ways in which they operate.

PROGRAMME AND PRODUCT
which looks at the ways in which arts programmes are put together and the factors which influence the programming decisions.

MANAGING AND RUNNING A VENUE
which looks at management options, staffing, and revenue costs.

SPACES FOR THE ARTS

TYPES OF VENUE
Most existing arts buildings fall into one of three main categories:
- Theatres, opera houses, concert halls and recital rooms for the presentation of drama, opera and dance and for listening to music. These are all performance-based buildings;

- Art galleries for the display of paintings, sculpture, photography and craft and art works. These buildings are exhibition-based;

- Arts centres which provide facilities for a range of activities and a mix of art forms. These buildings have a mixed base.

The more recently completed arts buildings and those which are currently being planned fit less easily into these categories. Increasingly, the spaces which make up a traditional theatre or gallery now constitute only the core of a new arts facility. Theatres, concert halls and art galleries are extending their facilities to provide for classes and groups working together, rehearsal and practice areas, studio space, and rooms for education work. Dance centres, visual arts centres, music centres and media centres are beginning to be developed. What is changing is not so much the nature of the individual spaces which are required (though many of the main spaces are becoming less formal and more flexible) but how these spaces are put together and what additional facilities are provided.

HOW THE DIFFERENT TYPES OF VENUES OPERATE
The way a building operates has an effect on both the design of the main spaces and the range of ancillary accommodation which needs to be provided. Performance-based buildings all operate according to one of a number of basic formats. Exhibition spaces tend to follow one of two main patterns of operation. Arts centres and the more specialist art-form based centres normally incorporate both performance and exhibition spaces which are run in accordance with one of the formats relating to those two uses. They also offer a range of other activities relating to their particular style and objectives. Theatres, concert halls, galleries, etc. may incorporate some elements of the arts centre and/or specialist centre as well as their main performance or exhibition elements.

PERFORMANCE-BASED BUILDINGS
There is a wide range of building types, within this general category. A performance-based building could be anything from an international opera house to an adapted village hall.

Performance spaces are also found in non-arts buildings - in civic centres, leisure centres, schools, community buildings and in rooms in pubs.

Whatever the size or situation, the basic operational formats remain the same. They are:

- Producing Venues

- Touring (or Receiving) Venues

- Multiple Use Venues

PRODUCING VENUES
These venues house companies which produce their own work. They present this work either in 'repertory' when each production runs for a limited period with consecutive performances, or in 'repertoire' when a number of productions are held and presented intermittently over a period. Many also produce work to tour.

Venues which normally operate on this basis include:
- the main regional theatres (with the repertory system);

- the building-based opera and dance companies (with the repertoire system);

- the national drama companies (with the repertoire system);

- the small 'building-based' companies which specialise in new work (with the repertory system).

TOURING (OR RECEIVING) VENUES
These venues present work generated elsewhere. Each production runs for a limited period before moving on to a similar venue.

Venues which normally operate on this basis include:
- the large touring theatres in the major conurbations;

- most concert halls, though with much shorter runs (often one performance). They may also provide a working base for a company which gives some performances at the base venue but also tours;

- theatres which take in productions and run them for as long as the box office takings permit. Most of these are in London's West End.

MULTIPLE USE VENUES
These venues present a mix of productions (drama, dance, music), a mix of events (performances, events, activities) and/or a mix of work produced by a resident company and work bought in from elsewhere.

Venues which normally operate in this way include:
- most performance-based arts centres;

- performance facilities linked to schools and universities;

- purpose-built multiple use facilities.

Venues which operate mainly as repertory, repertoire or receiving venues may also put on a mix of productions and events to extend their range and/or increase their income.

EXHIBITION SPACES
The majority of publicly funded art galleries are primarily concerned with the collection, preservation and display of permanent collections. While many of these collections include works by living artists, the main opportunities for seeing a range of current art come through galleries which put on changing exhibitions rather than those with more permanent collections.

Exhibition spaces which show contemporary painting, sculpture, photographs, craft and other art work can be accommodated in a range of venues. For example:
- many of the galleries housing permanent collections have some space dedicated to showing exhibitions;

- there are a few galleries which are solely devoted to the promotion and display of exhibitions. Some of these specialise in a single area of work such as photography;

- there are also a few small galleries run by groups of artists. These may be linked to studio facilities or workshops;

- most arts centres have some space for showing art works, though only a proportion of these spaces is equipped to take exhibitions which need controlled environmental conditions and a high level of security. Centres specialising in the visual arts normally have a range of well equipped exhibition spaces;

- public buildings, such as libraries, town halls and community centres, often have spaces available for showing exhibitions, as do some commercial buildings.

Most of the specialist galleries mount exhibitions which are researched and put together in house or directly commissioned. Some of these exhibitions are subsequently made available to galleries with comparable facilities.

Exhibitions specially designed for touring purposes are produced at the South Bank Centre for the Arts Council's Touring Exhibition Service. This service produces a graded range of exhibitions. Those in the upper grades are only made available to exhibition spaces which offer good environmental and security control systems.

Exhibitions are also mounted and toured by a number of cultural and design-based organisations.

Most exhibition spaces operate on a mixed basis, mounting some of their own exhibitions and buying in some touring work.

ARTS CENTRES
Arts centres provide for a range of activities to take place within the same building. They usually cater for a number of art forms and for different ways of practising those forms. They provide exhibition space alongside performance space, studios and workshops. They present art to the

public and provide facilities to draw the public into participating in the arts.

Types of centres
Arts centres can comprise a group of buildings offering facilities comparable to those found in individual arts buildings. For instance the Barbican Centre has a full scale concert hall, theatre, studio theatre and gallery, all within a single building. Warwick University Arts Centre also offers a similar range of facilities but in separate buildings, grouped together to form an arts complex.

There are a number of local authority purpose-built centres. These are, in the main, performance-based with multi-purpose halls designed to take a range of middle scale work which does not require highly specialised facilities. Some of these buildings are designed to cater also for sports and community uses.

Most arts centre are on a smaller scale. Some of them provide the only arts resource for the surrounding area, others offer community-based facilities at a local level or seek to present alternatives to the existing provision in town and city centres.

organising courses and workshops, activities for schools, holiday programmes for young people and outreach work for those who cannot easily travel to take part in arts events. They also provide residencies for artists who work with the local community while continuing to develop their own creative work. The workshops, courses and residencies cover drama, dance, music, the visual arts, crafts, photography, film, video and creative writing. Rooms need to be provided, or the main spaces made sufficiently adaptable, to accommodate this range of activities.

The buildings serve an additional function as a meeting place, somewhere for people to go to pass the time or meet like-minded groups. This means spaces need to be provided for people to gather in - bars and cafes, with 'ad hoc' entertainment; creche facilities for workshop and course related activities; and rooms for local groups to use for meetings and activities.

Arts centres are the most individual form of arts building. They are often started by a group of enthusiasts, with a particular interest, and located in 'found space' (i.e. an existing building which has to be converted for arts use). While the arts centres taken together cover a very wide range of

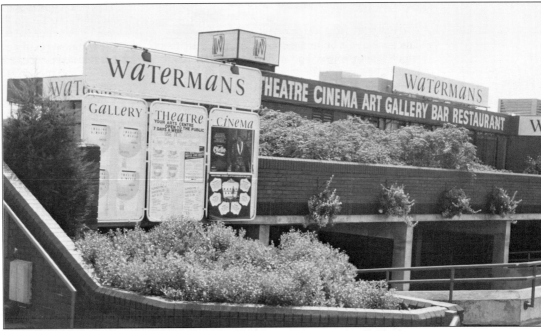

Watermans Arts Centre, Brentford (photograph by Rob Bell)

While many arts centre programmes are strongly linked to performance and exhibitions, these centres do not just offer smaller scale theatre and gallery spaces. They aim to provide a wider range of work, with a closer contact between the artists and their audiences and with a greater emphasis on the contemporary and experimental. They also seek to work across the art forms through festivals, thematic programmes and integrated projects. This is reflected in the type of spaces provided - they tend to be more flexible and informal than those in a traditional theatre or gallery.

Most centres aim to encourage wide public participation in the arts in all its forms. To this end, many arts centres put a high priority on

interests, an individual centre may concentrate on a more limited range of activities linked to the spaces it has available, the skills of those involved, and the interests of the local community.

SPECIALIST CENTRES FOR THE ARTS
There is another form of arts centre being developed which concentrates on providing for a range of activities linked to a single art form. For instance, a dance centre might include a performance space and provide a base for a professional dance company. The facilities for the company could include rehearsal spaces and practice rooms which could be shared with other dancers and dance groups in the area, as well as providing spaces for dance classes. Such a centre might also act as a meeting place for dancers, serve as a

resource unit for the local community and provide a working base for a dance 'animateur' whose job is to stimulate interest in dance in the surrounding area. It might also include a medical unit for dance-related injuries.

Similarly, a music centre could provide: a concert hall or smaller music performance space; rehearsal facilities for orchestras, for groups and bands, and for individual musicians; recording facilities; and a studio space equipped for electronic music.

A visual arts centre could provide: gallery spaces for exhibitions of contemporary art and photography; artists' studios; print and photography workshops; film and video making facilities; cinema spaces and areas for group work.

While those working in these centres share much of the arts centre philosophy in seeking to integrate practice with performance and professional artists with students and the public, they also aim to provide a more specialised environment in terms of staff, work and facilities. Examples of centres of this type include: The Cornerhouse, Manchester (visual arts); Yorkshire Dance Centre, Leeds; and The Waterfront, Norwich (live music).

PROGRAMME AND PRODUCT

The design of a building is based on the activities which it is to house. The activities have, therefore, to be carefully defined before any design work can start. This requires an outline programme to be produced.

DRAWING UP A PROGRAMME

Every arts facility, however broadly based, needs to have an arts policy which sets out its aims and establishes its reason for existence. This policy provides the base on which the programme is developed.

In drawing up the programme, a number of objectives have to be met. These include:
- to present the arts to the highest possible standard in accordance with the overall policy;
- to work within the given financial parameters;
- to respond to the needs and expectations of the user groups and the funding bodies.

These three criteria contain elements of conflict within them which have to be resolved if a venue is to operate successfully.

Most arts venues aim to provide a programme which offers a range of arts work and a mix of activities within the limits of its terms of operation. This can be achieved by mixing elements in a number of different areas. For instance:
- Presentation and participation.

  Presentation events include the whole range of performances - drama, dance, opera, music or any combination of these art forms,

as well as exhibitions and films. Participatory events include classes and workshops as well as individual studio work, both in the performance arts and in the visual arts.

- General and specialised.

  Some events appeal to a wide cross-section of the population while others attract smaller, more specialist audiences. Both types of activity have a place in a broadly based programme.

- Profit making and subsidised.

  Some types of event are more profitable than others. Profit-making events are those which bring in more income than they cost to put on. A traditional opera, for instance, can fill a large auditorium to capacity but it is rarely profitable because it involves a large number of performers, orchestra and stage crew as well as sets, costumes, etc. An individual performer might attract a smaller audience but still be more profitable.

- Commercial and service.

  There is scope in most arts venues to include activities in the programme for mainly commercial reasons. For example, the premises could be made available for conferences, receptions, trade promotions, parties and meetings. Events such as discotheques, fairs and markets can be mounted on a commercial basis.

  Other facilities may be provided on a service basis (e.g. creche, after-school and holiday activities, special events for those who cannot normally get to the building). Some charges can be made for such activities but the reason they are included in the programme is to provide a service, not to make money.

- Individual or group.

  Artists and people interested in a particular art form need opportunities to work together (e.g. orchestral groups, bands, actors' classes). They also welcome the opportunity to work on an individual basis (e.g. a musician who has no alternative practice space, a dancer between jobs, a painter, craftsperson, photographer or sculptor with no suitable studio space).

THE ARTS PRODUCT

The main element of most arts venue activities is the presentation of art to the public in the form of plays, ballet and other dance productions, opera, mime, concerts, song recitals, films, displays and exhibitions. All this is known as the 'arts product'. Such product is either produced by an arts company housed in the venue or bought in. In drawing up a programme, both the availability and the cost of the product need to be considered. The cost of the product has to be set against the potential income. Where the cost is greater than the income, some form of subsidy is required if the work is to be shown. Most venues need subsidy to help provide a balanced programme. Defining the product which is appropriate for any particular venue and establishing whether it is likely to be available, is a job which requires experience.

Though there is a wide range of product available, there may not always be enough of any one particular style or scale to satisfy the demand which means that the scope for new provision is limited in some areas. The existing large touring theatres, for instance, form a recognised grid across the country, with one such theatre in each of the major conurbations. A new facility is unlikely to be included in the grid and receive major touring product unless it has a catchment area which is not covered by any of the existing theatres.

The supply of more traditionally presented work for smaller and medium sized venues is also limited, though some new touring companies are aiming to fill this need.

Small rural arts centres which want a range of product to appeal to a broad cross-section of the local population may also experience problems. Several of the Regional Arts Associations with large rural areas are currently working to provide more product of this sort.

THE RELATIONSHIP BETWEEN PRODUCT AND SIZE OF VENUE
The product which can be shown in a venue is determined to some extent by the size and scale of the performance spaces.

Venues tend to be categorised on the basis of seating capacity. Though this is partly an administrative convenience to enable venues to be slotted into appropriate touring programmes, it also relates to the potential levels of income which can be expected from ticket sales and the size and overall volume of the performance spaces.

The terms 'small scale', 'middle scale' and 'large scale' are used, but these are not definitive. The following figures give a guide to how they are used.

Small scale 100 - 500 seats

Medium scale 500 - 1200 seats

Large scale 1200 - 3000 seats

When opera and music are being discussed, the term 'small scale' can refer to a venue of 600 - 1000 seats.

THE ECONOMICS OF SCALE
Within the given scale, the higher the seating capacity the more likely the venue is to be viable. For instance, a theatre of 1,200 seats operating in the large scale touring market will be at an economic disadvantage in comparison with a theatre of 2,000 as the cost of the productions remains constant. This assumes that the larger

theatre can fill its auditorium on a regular basis, without having to lower its seat prices.

For a very small venue (or a medium sized venue which wants to show large scale product), economics become a matter of assessing the amount of subsidy available for each production.

THE NEED FOR SUBSIDY
To operate, most arts companies and venues need money in addition to that which can be earned from the box office, entry fees, sale of work and other arts activities.

The need for subsidy relates to the nature of the arts. The arts product is individual and results either from the co-operative efforts of a fairly large number of people or the intensive work of a single person over a long period. The number of people who can particiapte in an arts event at any one time is also limited.

Any organisation which sets up a new arts facility on the basis that it can break even if managed efficiently is likely to be disappointed though there are ways of improving the income/expenditure balance. These relate in the main to introducing (and designing for) a range of ancillary uses which are income earning - for example by including general entertainment, popular films, cabaret style events, discos etc. in the programme; letting out facilities for conferences, receptions, meetings and parties; setting aside space for commercially based retail and service outlets.

SUBSIDISING ARTS COMPANIES
If a venue is to operate as a 'producing venue', creating its own work, it has to provide a base for a producing arts company, such as a drama company, dance group, orchestra or opera company.

These companies need to be financed. Many existing arts companies receive grants from the Arts Council, the Regional Arts Associations or the Scottish or Welsh Arts Councils. Such grants are discretionary, and in the present financial situation it is difficult for a new company to attract finance from these sources. Where an organisation such as a local authority or development group plans to provide a new facility which creates some, if not all, of its own product, it is worth their considering whether an existing company can be attracted to move into the new facility. The Barbican Centre, for example, provided a new home for the Royal Shakespeare Company, whilst the Sadler's Wells Royal Ballet has recently been attracted to move to Birmingham. Opportunities also exist on a smaller scale for rehousing locally-based arts companies or attracting others into an area by offering good working facilities. The grants the companies receive would not necessarily move with them, so it is important that any discussions regarding a proposed change of base include all the relevant funding bodies.

SUBSIDISING AN ARTS VENUE
It is more likely that a new arts facility will be

planned as a 'receiving venue', buying in product which is generated elsewhere.

In this case, much of the product it receives is already subsidised through grants paid directly to the touring companies. It is unlikely that any additional subsidy will be available from the arts organisations except to help with special events.

Even with subsidised product, few venues break even. Many venues are supported by local authorities. Additional money often has to be sought from the private sector through sponsorship, donations and friends' arrangements.

(Further information is given in the chapter 'Finance and Funding'.)

MANAGING AND RUNNING A VENUE

The way a building is to be run and managed affects the amount of administrative space to be provided and the organisation of this space. It is also important to work out the overall costs of running the venue before design work starts. Any amendments which need to be made-either to reduce the amount or scale of provision or to increase the income-earning potential-can then be incorporated into the design brief.

MANAGEMENT STRUCTURES

Most arts organisations are either independently run and managed, or linked in some way to a local authority. Some arts centres and smaller performance facilities are linked to an educational body (university, school or college), whilst a small number of theatres are commercially owned and managed.

FORMATS FOR INDEPENDENT ORGANISATIONS

Independent organisations are normally run either as companies limited by guarantee or as trusts, with boards of directors or trustees. Board members are responsible for defining policy, overseeing finance, setting management objectives and determining priorities.

A few arts groups are run as co-operatives which means that everybody involved in the organisation has equal responsibility for the way it operates and an equal share in its assets. This is only appropriate for small groups with interests in common.

The bibliography lists a number of publications which define the legal status of the various formats and the responsibilities of board members.

LOCAL AUTHORITY OPTIONS

Where a local authority is considering providing a new arts facility, it has the option of either setting it up as an independent company or trust or of running it within its own organisation.

The Local Government and Housing Act 1989 regulates local authorities' interests in companies so any authority considering the first option needs to take the implications of this act into account. The Act limits the independence of

certain companies which receive money from a local authority and controls the disposal of assets (including leasehold agreements). The National Council for Voluntary Organisations has published a guide to the Local Government and Housing Act 1989 entitled 'The Conduct of Local Government'.

If the arts facility is owned and managed by the local authority it has all the advantages of being part of a large organisation with a range of resources. Management functions such as building maintenance, personnel administration, publicity, marketing and computer services can be undertaken within the authority and particular areas of expertise (architectural, financial, legal) can be provided as necessary. The responsibility for arts and arts facilities is normally held by the Department of Recreation and Leisure Services where staff have experience of operating venues (e.g. sports halls, swimming pools and leisure facilities).

The disadvantages relate in the main to flexibility and accountability. Some local authorities have experienced problems in fitting arts administrators and support staff into their existing structures and some arts staff have found the working practices too restrictive. There can also be problems relating to the nature of the arts. Works of art (whether performance-based or exhibition material) can be controversial either in the ideas which they express or in the means they use to express them. Some local authorities find it preferable to distance themselves, in structural terms, from the arts organisations they set up, giving the financial support but enabling them to operate without any direct control. This is usually done by setting up a trust to run the organisation with a given number of local authority members serving either 'ex-officio' or as nominees of the authority.

Local authorities are also beginning to consider leasing arts facilities to commercial management teams. This can be an option where a performance venue has a commercial potential or where the arts facility forms part of a larger complex. In such situations, the terms of the lease need to state how the facility is to be used, possibly setting aside a given amount of time for specific productions or a non-commercially based programme.

OPTIONS FOR EDUCATIONAL INSTITUTIONS

In the past, universities and other educational institutions found it easier to accommodate flexible management and staffing requirements into their organisations, with much of the support staff being recruited from the student bodies. In recent years, cut-backs in university finance have put pressure on these facilities. Setting up an independent trust, which is able to seek additional finance from outside sources, could be a solution.

Where arts centres or performance spaces are linked to schools, they have mainly been managed as part of the school. The only problem with this way of operating is that it usually requires one member of staff to have a joint teaching and administrative role and it may be difficult to find someone with the right balance of skills and interests.

having to maintain the building, it separates potential conflicts of interest (arts companies tend to postpone expenditure on necessary maintenance rather than cut back on arts activi-

Edward Alleyn Hall, Dulwich College, London (photograph by Martin Charles for the 'Architects Journal')

COMMERCIAL OPTIONS
Commercially owned arts buildings are nearly all large and medium scale touring theatres. They are mostly grouped together to form units for a range of touring product. (For example, there is a group of medium sized traditional style theatres which take productions before they go to the London commercial theatres.) Some commercial entertainment-based organisations lease buildings from local authorities. In some cases, the leasing agreement carries an undertaking to promote certain types of work or make a given amount of space available to specified uses. (See 'Local Authority Options' above.)

SEPARATING BUILDING OWNERSHIP FROM ARTS MANAGEMENT
With both independent arts bodies and those which are part of large organisations, it is possible to separate the ownership of the building from the responsibility for what goes on inside it. A producing theatre company, for instance, can be constituted for the sole purpose of mounting dramatic productions. The building it occupies, both as its working base and as the venue for its performances, can be owned by a separate company or trust set up for that purpose or can be retained by the organisation (e.g. a local authority) which originally built it. In such a case the building will be leased to the arts company. This solution has a number of advantages. It releases the arts company from the pressures of

ties), and allows board members to relate their interests and expertise more closely to one particular area. Where the building is owned by an independent trust it needs to be given sufficient resources to maintain the building. These can be provided through an annual allocation of funds, through the rent paid by the arts company or in the form of an endowment.

Where an existing company is undertaking a major building project, it may be worth considering forming a separate trust to raise the finance and carry out the building project.

Legal advice should be taken before separating responsibilities so that potential problems can be avoided. Areas to watch are charitable status, independence from government controls on local authority capital expenditure and borrowing, and the ability to reclaim VAT on building costs.

STAFFING AN ARTS ORGANISATION
In staffing an arts venue two main areas need to be provided for: the provision of the art and the running of the organisation and building.

In an organisation which houses a producing company (or a group of artists producing their own work) the staff are often divided into the artistic staff and the administrative staff. A producing theatre, for instance, has two senior staff: the artistic director, responsible for the nature, quality and style of the work undertaken; and the administrator, responsible for the organisation, staffing, budgeting, marketing, catering, etc. The artistic director normally holds the senior position and acts as the chief executive. He/she is responsible for the performers, designer, technicians and stage staff. The administrator has a team of staff related to the running of the organisation and building.

In a receiving venue, where the arts product is bought in, the main area of responsibility is one of management, but the person in charge also has to define an artistic policy for the venue and to plan and develop the arts programme. This person is normally known as the director.

In an organisation where there is a strong element of participation, the administrative team needs the support of a number of creative artists and people skilled in project and workshop work. The term 'animateurs' is used to describe those involved in organising projects and stimulating related activities.

SALARIES
Salaries in the independent arts organisations tend to be low though efforts are being made to improve them by drawing comparisons with similar posts in local authority and commercially managed organisations. In 1988, the National Association of Arts Centres (now the Arts Development Association) set up a working party to study the remuneration levels of people working in arts centres throughout the country. The Association subsequently drew up a set of guidelines recommending a minimum salary level for any arts centre chief officer (£12,960 up to July 1990) and linking other positions to local authority grades and salary scales.

Because of the low salaries and the demands made on a person's time and energy, running an arts organisation has traditionally been regarded as a young person's job, with those who do it moving on to other things as their personal responsibilities increase. This had led to a shortage of experienced managerial staff which means that better salaries and good working conditions have to be offered to recruit people at this level.

An indication of current salaries, across a range of arts posts, can be gained by reading the 'situations vacant' pages in the press. The main publications for arts vacancies are 'The Stage' and the Arts and Media sections of 'The Guardian'.

THE COSTS OF RUNNING AN ARTS VENUE
Once a building is open and operating, the expenditure falls into three main areas: financing the programme, providing the administration, and running and maintaining the building.

FINANCING THE ARTS PROGRAMME
Putting on a programme of arts activities costs money. Where work is being produced by the venue, expenditure is incurred in salaries (per-formers, artists, production and technical staff) and in materials. Where work is brought in, it has to be paid for - as a fee, a proportion of the 'take', or a combination of both. With participatory activities artists are needed to work with the local community either as 'artists in residence' or commissioned for particular work (possibly for regular classes, for a series of workshops or for one-off events). This means expenditure is incurred on salaries and/or fees and on the necessary materials for their work.

PROVIDING THE ADMINISTRATION
Arts buildings require people to run them and organise the activities. In addition to the salaries and related staff costs and benefits, staff require equipment and budget allocations to carry out their work. Telephone and postage bills can be high in an arts venue. The publicity and advertising costs should not be underestimated (a guide figure is about 10% of the cost of buying in the product).

RUNNING AND MAINTAINING THE BUILDING
The costs of services - to provide heating, ventilation, lighting, etc. - form a significant part of the revenue budget. Water rates and a proportion of the commercial rates have to be paid. The building and equipment require regular cleaning and servicing, both on a day-to-day basis and on a scheduled basis for more major work. Routine maintenance is required and an allowance needs to be made to replace fittings and equipment as they wear out or become obsolete. The budget needs to take account of the costs of redecoration and refurbishment, security and insurance. (See page 26, 'The Building in Use'.)

SITES AND BUILDINGS

This chapter draws together a range of information relating to finding and acquiring a site or building.

It is divided into two parts:

NEW BUILDINGS, CONVERSIONS AND IMPROVEMENTS
which outlines the advantages and disadvantages of each approach and the processes involved. The text on 'Conversions' looks at the various types of buildings which may be available and identifies their main strengths and weaknesses for arts use.

FINDING, CHECKING AND ACQUIRING SUITABLE PROPERTY
which looks at the location of arts facilities, ways of finding suitable property, forms of ownership, planning legislation, property values, mortgages and insurance. It also lists the main checks which need to be made before a site or building is acquired.

NEW BUILDINGS, CONVERSIONS AND IMPROVEMENTS
Where there is a choice between constructing a new building and improving or converting an existing building it is worth considering which

option best suits the purpose.

Organisations with some experience of planning and building tend to consider constructing a new building more readily than those working in the arts. Local authorities, government departments, development corporations, educational institutions, and commercial building and development firms all fall within this category.

Small, independent or voluntary organisations tend to opt for the job of improving what they have or of converting an existing building.

Each of these solutions has some points in its favour and some inherent problems.

ADVANTAGES AND DISADVANTAGES OF EACH APPROACH

NEW BUILDINGS

Advantages
New buildings offer all the advantages of a purpose-designed product:
- They provide the spaces which are needed, and only those which are needed, relating spaces to activities;

- They offer a wide range of design options which can take account of new developments and accommodate a range of uses;

- They can make use of more sophisticated technology to improve facilities for the arts, control the environmental conditions, provide flexibility, increase security and reduce running costs.

Disadvantages
- Suitable sites are difficult to find;

- The process of designing and building is time-consuming;

- A new building is generally a more expensive option (though this is due in some part to the fact that the end product offers better facilities with fewer compromises).

CONVERSIONS

Advantages
- It is often possible to find an attractive building occupying a good, accessible site. Some are subject to planning contraints which reduce their commercial value (and, therefore, their selling price);

- Some of the buildings available are interesting in their own right, with a strong visual identity and well-liked by the public;

- Most existing buildings can be converted more cheaply than the equivalent space can be built;

- Some existing buildings can be brought into use at a relatively low cost and then phased improvement work can be carried out as the

necessary funding is raised.

Disadvantages
- Nearly all converted buildings have elements of compromise in their use. Activities have to be adapted to suit the spaces available;

- Existing buildings rarely offer the right mix of large and small scale spaces;

- Converted buildings are often more expensive to maintain and improve. In an old building, particularly a listed building, work on the building structure and services tends to be non-standard, often requiring special materials and specialist craftsmen;

- Given the same standards, the running costs are higher;

- Access and parking can present problems when considering old buildings in tight town centre sites.

IMPROVEMENTS
Most existing arts buildings offer scope for improvement. Those with sufficient surrounding land to accommodate some additions obviously offer more flexibility of approach.

Advantages
- The facility is already established in its location and those who use it know its strengths and weaknesses;

- Continuity can be maintained;

- The work can be phased and it may be possible to continue using the building while work is in hand;

- It will often be the least expensive solution.

Disadvantages
- Not all problems are soluble;

- The basic structure remains the same - for example old foundations or deteriorating brickwork.

PLANNING NEW BUILDINGS
New buildings, in theory, are the ideal solution to housing the arts because they are designed to accommodate defined needs, are able to take advantage of others' experience and make use of up-to-date materials and technology. There are examples of new buildings across the country which provide stimulating and sympathetic environments for the arts which they house. Many of these have attracted interest far beyond that envisaged by their planners and have rapidly become focal points for their surrounding areas. Some others have been less successful.

One of the problems is that of turning ideas (which can be fluid) into built form (which is, by nature, more or less static). When a building project is being designed, ideas have to be clarified so that decisions can be taken. If the

INTERIORS AND EXTERIORS OF NEW BUILDINGS

Exterior: Theatre Royal, Plymouth (photograph by the Cement And Concrete Association)

Exterior: View of the first phase of the new Wilde Theatre at South Hill Park arts centre, Bracknell, taken from the garden of the existing house (photograph by Alastair Haines)

Interior: A dance workshop in the auditorium of the Wilde Theatre (photograph by Peter Cook)

Interior: The main auditorium of the Theatre Royal, Plymouth, showing the ceiling in the raised position to give maximum seating capacity

Exterior: View of the Minerva Theatre, Chichester, showing the theatre, restaurant and clubroom (photograph by Timothy Soar)

Interior: The foyer and circulation areas of the Minerva Theatre (photograph by Timothy Soar)

initiating organisation attempts to fudge important issues (e.g. about how certain spaces are to be used) the designer will be forced to take the necessary decisions to progress the project. These decisions may, or may not, be in line with the organisation's actual requirements.

When a group is being rehoused, there is a temptation to try to recreate an existing space which 'works' without seeking to identify the elements which contribute towards its success or recognising the adjustments which are made as part of everyday life. New buildings cannot recreate 'found space' (e.g. as in a warehouse). Where the strength of a space is its 'ad hoc' and temporary quality, very careful consideration needs to be given to a move to any new facility.

Because they start with a blank sheet, some organisations expect their buildings to achieve the impossible. Activities which are incompatible do not mix happily merely because they are put into a new building. Special provision has to be made and compromises have to be accepted.

Costs need to be carefully controlled. Many new buildings suffer because they are subject to cuts at a late stage in the design process, or when building work is underway. This inevitably means that some important elements have to be omitted and/or the quality of the materials and fittings has to be reduced. A more satisfactory outcome is achieved by planning for a more economical building at the design stage.

CONVERTING BUILDINGS TO ARTS USE

There is now an established tradition of putting arts activities into redundant churches, schools, warehouses, etc. which has led people to assume that all old buildings of any interest can have an arts use. This is not the case.

However attractive a redundant building may appear, it is essential that it is assessed, first and foremost, in terms of the provision it can make for the arts. Unless there is a clear policy and artistic rationale for its use, it will end up hampering rather than developing the arts. While many attractive old buildings have been successfully converted to arts use, too many others have resulted in providing the arts with 'inappropriate facilities in inappropriate premises in inaccessible locations'.*

Purpose-built arts facilities which have fallen into disuse may also appear to offer excellent opportunities for the arts. It is tempting to assume that, because a building once had an active arts role, it can be successfully brought back into arts use. It may, however, have become redundant for very good reasons. The area of population it served could have changed or the facilities it offered could have become inappropriate as the arts developed. Some arts buildings, even some visually attractive ones, were poorly designed for their purpose in the first place. It is important, therefore, to assess a disused theatre, gallery or concert hall as carefully as any other building.

THE ARTS USE POTENTIAL OF REDUNDANT BUILDINGS

While a wide range of buildings has been converted to house the arts, experience shows that some types are more appropriate for arts use in general than others and some relate better to one particular art form. The following text lists some of the main building categories and outlines their strengths and weaknesses.

The categorisation of building types and related arts uses is developed in a study 'Planning the Arts Centre Building' undertaken by architect Peter Eley for the Royal Society of Arts in 1986.

Theatres

There is still a large number of Victorian and Edwardian theatres remaining across the country. Those which are still in use as social clubs and bingo halls are often in a fairly good state of repair, with much of the interior intact. Others, which have been given over to less sympathetic uses such as stores or showrooms, have probably lost most of the original interiors (i.e. stage area, pit, stalls rake and possibly the upper seating levels and access stairs) as have those which have been converted into multi-screen cinemas.

Even where an existing theatre is in a reasonable state of repair, it is likely that a good deal of work will be required to bring it up to present day standards. Few old theatres provide adequate backstage and front of house facilities for current requirements.

Churches and Chapels

Because of changes in where people live and the decline in the numbers attending church services, redundant church buildings are probably one of the most readily available sources of space in town and city areas. Churches and chapels have been converted into arts centres, theatres and concert halls. They have many good attributes. They are usually soundly built, with a strong local presence, and well located. Many offer a good sized main space with sufficient height for a performance space or exhibition facility. The acoustics are often very acceptable as far as music is concerned (though they may be less good for speech).

The disadvantages are the limited amount of ancillary accommodation offered, high maintenance and running costs, and problems with sound insulation. Churches normally provide one main space with one or two small rooms. The surrounding site is not always available for development. They are notoriously difficult to heat and expensive to maintain. The large windows make insulation difficult (blocking them in may spoil the appearance of the building while merely screening them means that exterior noise intrudes on the arts use).

Churches designed for use by the non-conformist denominations tend to provide better spaces than those originally built by the Roman Catholic or

*(Rick Welton, Director of the Arts Development Association.)

INTERIORS AND EXTERIORS OF CONVERTED BUILDINGS

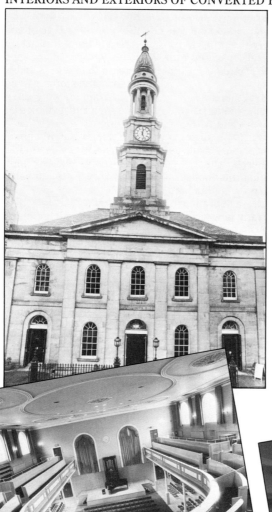

Exterior: The Queen's Hall, Edinburgh (photograph by Sean Hudson)

Exterior: The Cornerhouse film and exhibition centre, Manchester (photograph by Ged Murray)

Interior: The Queen's Hall, converted to concert use (photograph by Sean Hudson)

Exterior: The Corn Exchange, Cambridge (photograph by the City of Cambridge, Department of Planning, Photograph Department)

Interior: One of the smaller gallery spaces in the converted Cornerhouse building

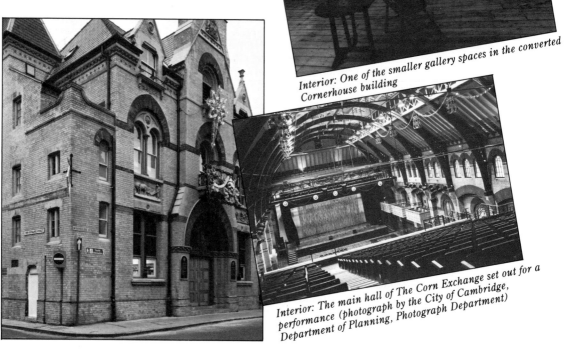

Interior: The main hall of The Corn Exchange set out for a performance (photograph by the City of Cambridge, Department of Planning, Photograph Department)

Church of England authorities, as they often have a more open format. The traditional gothic style church, with a central aisle delineated by pillars supporting an arched roof structure is very difficult to use successfully.

Schools
With the continuing fall in the birthrate and the re-organisation of education provision, redundant school buildings are likely to provide a source of space well into the future. They can be of any age or size, though the larger, better maintained schools are more likely to be retained within the education provision for an area. Schools share some of the advantages of church buildings in that they are usually well built and well located. In terms of the spaces they offer, the advantages and problems are opposite. While churches offer a good central space and limited ancillary accommodation, schools tend to have a large number of medium sized rooms, lots of corridor space and a small hall. The best schools for arts use are the older style (pre-1939) primary schools where the halls are more generous in their dimensions relative to the number of classrooms and the classrooms often open off the main space. Larger educational buildings tend to have long corridors with rows of doors opening off. Such a layout gives an impersonal feel to the complex, isolating the indvidual activities and mitigating against good internal communications. Reception areas, which are vital to the successful functioning of an arts facility often have to be built onto schools or carved out of the existing interiors.

Industrial and Commercial Buildings
This category covers a wide range of old buildings such as warehouses, breweries, mills, malthouses, and commodity exchange halls. Many of these are attractive buildings of historic interest, some of which may be listed.

It also includes more modern industrial buildings, redundant stores, showrooms and factories. With the change in retail provision some of the older style town centre shops are becoming redundant and several have been successfully converted to arts use. Though less attractive than the older style buildings, they are often well situated and easily accessible by public transport.

What many of these buildings have in common is good uncluttered space. Warehouses tend to have a common structure. An outer shell of loadbearing walls supports the roof and the interior floors are carried on a rows of columns. This means that the interior can be altered without too much difficulty to give the space and height which many arts activities require. These types of structures can provide good gallery spaces for contemporary art and sculpture. They normally have long blank walls uninterrupted by windows and enough interior space to accommodate services and allow flexibility in screening. Large objects can be brought into the building and moved around quite easily. The flat surfaced, windowless, box-like interior can also be adapted for music use. As these buildings offer both space and flexibility, there are few limitations as to their potential use. Many of the more success-

ful conversions make use of this type of building.

The main disadvantage lies in the costs which can be incurred. Older buildings may well have been empty for some time before the new use is proposed. Money will firstly have to be spent in making the structure safe and weatherproof. If the building is listed, specific materials will have to be used. The building will then provide a shell into which the arts provision and services have to be fitted. In some cases the interior will have to be virtually rebuilt. Insulation, both for sound and heat, can be a problem as these structures were built as storehouses and workplaces. They are unlikely to be provided with anything other than very basic services. Whereas some buildings in other categories can be brought into use and upgraded over a period of time, most of the buildings in this category require a substantial amount of money to be spent before they can be opened to the public.

Public Buildings
Reorganisations in local government and services lead to some public buildings becoming redundant. Included in this category are not only redundant town halls but a wide range of buildings such as libraries, courthouses, police stations, fire stations, swimming pools, clinics and even old gaols. (There are examples of each of these building types having been converted to arts use.)

As their original uses differ, so the range of spaces they offer varies from one building to another. In general, public buildings are well constructed and have been reasonably well maintained. They often become available soon after they have been vacated and so can be used on a temporary basis without much initial expenditure. The main disadvantages are the large number of small rooms relative to large spaces, the formality of the building style and of the interior layout, and their structural inflexibility.

Private Houses
Once again this is a very broad category covering any form of residence from a large country mansion standing in its own ground to a small house or country cottage. Each of these has been used to provide arts facilities.

Small groups of artists have taken over terraced houses to provide studios, print and photographic workshops or operating bases for touring companies. Houses such as these can still be relatively inexpensive to buy outright in areas which are no longer attractive for residential purposes but are centrally located and accessible.

In general, houses provide a lot of small to medium sized spaces (which make them good for studios and workshops), but few large scale open spaces. Mansions may provide rooms large enough for a gallery or performance space (though even a large ballroom will convert into a fairly tight auditorium) but these large spaces are counterbalanced by a very large number of smaller rooms. The overheads of running an arts venue based in houses of this type are very high.

IMPROVING EXISTING BUILDINGS

Much of the building work carried out on arts buildings relates to the improvement of existing buildings. At least half the arts organisations in this country occupy buildings which are over a hundred years old. Many of these were converted on limited budgets and have been maintained on an 'ad hoc' basis ever since. The buildings provided in the expansion years of the 1960s are also beginning to need refurbishing and improving to meet current requirements.

PLANNING THE IMPROVEMENT WORK

There is a genuine conflict of interest between the long-term need to provide and maintain good buildings for the arts and the more immediate pressures facing most arts administrators of keeping the show on the road on a year by year basis. When overall funding is limited it is difficult for arts administrators to take a longer term view and to resist the temptation of seeing the future of the building as someone else's problem.

Improvement work which is undertaken as a series of short-term responses to immediate problems is ineffective and costly over a longer period. It needs to be cumulative with each new element adding to what has already been achieved. This more positive approach requires planning.

Planning an improvement scheme is not so different from that planning in a new building project. The scale of work may be much smaller and the scope more limited, with fewer options to choose from, but the process of research, assessment and evaluation is still important. Proposed changes need to be thought through carefully, a brief has to be prepared, a design drawn up, and the necessary building work organised.

The initial assessment of how the organisation uses the building is very important. The problems could be related to the way the building is organised or to its programme of activities rather than to the building itself.

Alternatively, the building could have a number of inherent faults which mean that it will never provide a satisfactory venue however much work is done on it. In this case, it is better to put up with the building's inadequacies in the short term, while looking for an alternative which offers more scope for future development.

Any single alteration to the structure or layout of a building has an effect on the building as a whole. Whatever option is selected limits future choices. This means that the building (together with any surrounding land) needs to be considered as a whole and a plan for its overall improvement drawn up even when only a small part of it can be carried out.

Most buildings have an overall design concept and this should be respected when changes are made. Quite substantial sums of money were spent in the 1970s and early 1980s ripping out the 'improvements' which previous generations had

made to the Victorian and Edwardian buildings. Cleaning and restoring the original fabric of a building is often the most effective form of improving the look of a building in the long-term.

Once an improvement plan has been agreed, any subsequent work, however small, should be carried out in accordance with that plan. It will then contribute to the overall scheme and not risk blocking future development opportunities.

TAKING PROFESSIONAL ADVICE

Looking at a building in terms of space and function and identifying the potential for improvement in building terms is the job of an architect and/or specialist arts designer such as a theatre consultant. Even where there seems little possibility of raising any large amounts of capital finance, it is worth considering drawing up an outline plan of phased improvements so that small maintenance jobs can contribute to the long-term plan. It may also be possible to identify relatively inexpensive ways of improving the way the building functions.

The Arts Council has introduced a scheme offering grants towards the cost of feasibility studies relating to new buildings and building improvements. Smaller, community-based venues may also get help towards the cost of such a study through the RIBA's Community Architecture Projects Fund.

Working out a plan in this way has the advantage of involving a professionally qualified designer in the project. Many people feel that small jobs (including extensions and structural alterations) can be left to the local builder. Builders are not trained as designers. They normally carry out the work in accordance with a set of design instructions. If they are not given adequate instructions they have to rely on their previous experience as the basis for the current job. Arts buildings do not follow any standard building types and the obvious solutions are not always the most appropriate ones.

SMALL SCALE WORKS

Arts organisations are often able to take advantage of voluntary help or community service schemes which can be used to improve the building. Once again, such help needs to be carried out in accordance with an overall plan. Each individual project also needs to be planned to avoid one stage of the work undoing the previous stage (e.g. deciding that doors need ventilating grids fitted only after they have been hung and painted).

Where a building contractor is appointed, it is his responsibility to ensure that the specialist sub-contractors carry out their part of the work on time. Many 'self-help' schemes need to bring in the specialist trades (e.g. electricians, plumbers and heating engineers) to carry out the more difficult jobs. This work needs to be carefully coordinated so that it slots into the overall programme, with the right people turning up at the right time.

Any work undertaken needs to be related to the

anticipated length of use of a facility. Where an organisation has a short-term lease on a building or knows that its occupancy is limited, it is sensible to use techniques which make the building as useful and pleasant as possible, both cheaply and quickly.

Where a building has a continuing arts use, any work which is undertaken should be done with the future in mind. This means that the structure and fabric of the building has to be made good before it is altered, covered or painted. For example, if damp stains are merely painted out they continue to reappear until someone gets round to dealing with the cause of the problem.

FINANCING IMPROVEMENTS
Grants are available to help towards the cost of some improvement work - for example towards the cost of improving access for people with disabilities, promoting equal opportunities and furthering educational needs. Other areas of improvement could attract building-related monies or form the basis of an appeal or a sponsorship agreement.

Once an overall plan is established it is easier to take advantage of any opportunities which occur. Government funding programmes change their emphasis within their overall terms of reference, from time to time. It is worth trying to keep in touch with such initiatives as they may provide sources of funding. (See bibliography for sources of information.)

Changes in the system for controlling local authority capital finance, could lead to small capital grants being made available towards the end of the financial year as revenue underspend can now be used for capital purposes. (Local Government and Housing Act 1989.)

It is also worth keeping an eye on what is happening in the area. The closure, change of use or demolition of existing buildings can be a source of cheap, if not free, fittings (e.g. a sprung dance floor, cinema seating, screens, etc.).

FINDING, CHECKING AND ACQUIRING SUITABLE PROPERTY
If new provision is to be made or an existing organisation is to be rehoused, a site or a building, suitable for conversion, needs to be acquired. In identifying and selecting a possible site or building the overriding priority has to be its suitability for the proposed arts use.

FINDING A SITE OR BUILDING
There is no single source or agency responsible for listing vacant sites. At any one time, only a small proportion of the possible sites or buildings is on offer for sale, though others, which are potentially available, may be identified by looking around and asking questions.

The Department of the Environment maintains a central register of publicly owned land which is considered to be unused or underused. This is available for public inspection at any one of the Department's Regional Offices. Local Authorities

are also required to maintain registers of any underused land which they own. The DoE has recently introduced the PROD (Public Request to Order Disposal) scheme through which members of the public can ask the DoE to facilitate the sale of such land. In London, the London Residuary Body maintains a register of buildings and sites previously owned by the Greater London Council.

The old statutory authorities own large amounts of land, some of which is now regarded as being surplus to their requirements. British Rail, British Telecom, British Gas, the Electricity Boards and the Water Authorities all own sites across the country, many of them in town and city centres. With privatisation, more of these land holdings are coming onto the market.

The public bodies and the old statutory authorities also own buildings (stations, telephone exchanges, schools, etc.) which are surplus to their requirements.

Estate agents have details of land and buildings which are currently on the market. Some specialise in commercial and industrial sites while others make this a section of a general agency. An established local agent should be in touch with what is happening around his/her area and be aware of any land or buildings available for sale whether or not he/she is acting as the agent.

Members of the local environmental groups also keep an eye on what is going on in their own areas.

Some potentially suitable sites have buildings on them. Arts organisations have tended in the past to acquire buildings only where they can be converted to arts use. Some sites, however, are occupied by low value buildings which can be demolished or small buildings which can be extended. Others have buildings on them which have a value apart from the surrounding land. These could be sold and the remaining land used for an arts facility.

It is not always easy to find out who owns a particular site or building. It may be possible to identify the freeholder through the land register. Where the land is built on, the local authority may also be able to trace the ownership through rating records.

Increasingly, new facilities for the arts are being provided by taking advantage of opportunities offered by new developments. (Information is given later in this section in the chapter 'Planning Gain and Development Opportunities'.)

GETTING THE LOCATION RIGHT
Location is important for arts buildings. Accessibility and the nature of the surrounding area are both key factors.

Arts buildings need a context - a busy street, an established high density housing area, a tourist centre, etc. Most buildings benifit from a town or city centre site, well served by public transport and situated where people regularly walk by.

Town centre sites in small side streets, or cut off by traffic, prove difficult, as do those in nondescript suburban areas and areas with a predominately office or other day-time only commercial use.

Arts building are often open late into the evening so they need to be sited somewhere which is easy to get to and which is regarded as being reasonably safe. (Recent surveys show that women predominate at arts events. Research commissioned by the Arts Council's Touring department indicates that 55% of theatre and 69% of ballet attenders are women.) In city centres, the arts facility gains from being sited alongside late-opening restaurants and shops. Bus stops, as well as parking, need to be close and safely accessible. The late evening use also means that sites with adjacent housing should be avoided, as residents tend to object to the noise of people and cars, even if the building itself is well enough designed to stop its activities disturbing the area.

Where arts facilities are sited away from the main centres, the most successful of them are in areas which provide a context (for example, a university campus, canal or riverside, or park). This helps establish a style and offers pleasant surroundings for a day or evening outing.

SORTING OUT PLANNING PERMISSION

The use of land and buildings and the design of new buildings (and most extensions and additions to existing buildings) is controlled by the relevant local authority under the terms of the Town and Country Planning Legislation. Responsibility at a local level lies with the District and Borough councils.

These authorities have drawn up structure plans and local plans which set out how different areas within the district or borough are to be used. Many areas will be designated for a certain type of use - housing, light industry, commercial, open space, etc. Conservation areas and areas of special interest are also identified.

When a site is being considered, checks need to be made with the local authority to ensure that proposed uses are in line with the overall plan for the area. Similarly, with an existing building, planning permission is required if the proposed use differs from the existing use.

The planning aspects of a project need to be considered as soon as a possible site or building has been identified. Most local authority planning officers are very helpful during these early stages. They will advise on whether the proposed use appears to be in accordance with the local plan and on how the application should be presented.

The application is submitted on a form available from the local authority department and a fee is usually payable. Planning permission has to be agreed or refused within a set period (normally eight weeks). During this time, people with an interest in the proposed development have the right to comment. How far this right extends

depends on the scope of the development.

In order to obtain full planning permission, detailed proposals with plans of any building or conversion work have to be submitted. However, it is possible to apply for outline planning permission at a much earlier stage. This will establish whether the site or building can be used for the activities proposed and the extent to which it can be developed. Once outline permission has been granted, the local authority is bound by its decision.

The permission may be subject to certain conditions. These could relate to the use of the proposed building (e.g. placing limits on the number of late-night performances) or to the design of the building (e.g. limiting the height or specifying what materials are to be used).

As arts buildings seek to increase the range and mix of their activities, they may find that more specialised forms of planning agreement are needed. Some uses may be acceptable, while others cause problems. One element in the proposed use could result in the whole application being rejected. It is, therefore, worth consulting the planning department at an early stage so that some form of planning agreement can be worked out. The local authority may wish to continue monitoring the uses or may establish a range which will allow flexibility within given parameters.

The right to apply for planning permission is not restricted to the owners of a building. This means that the planning requirements for buildings or sites can be checked out before any detailed work is done or any commitments are made. Where there is an element of doubt about permission being given for the uses proposed, it is advisable to put in an application for outline planning permission before the site or building is purchased. The contract to purchase can be made subject to the necessary planning permission being granted.

WAYS OF ACQUIRING A BUILDING

A site or property may be offered on a freehold or leasehold basis. Certain properties could be available for rent.

RENTING A PROPERTY

This can only be regarded as a short-term option e.g. to obtain the use of a building while other premises are being converted or constructed. Its disadvantages are: tenure is not guaranteed other than for an initial period; the rent may be increased at stated intervals; the value of any improvements made by the tenant is lost when the property reverts to the landlord; and the scope for alterations is very limited.

LEASING A PROPERTY

When property is offered leasehold it reverts to the freeholder at the end of the stated period of tenure. The terms on which a lease is offered vary. Some agreements give the leaseholder the right to use the property over a long period in return for a minimal ground rent once the initial purchase price has been paid. In other cases the purchase price is supplemented by an annual rental which may be increased at stated intervals. The freeholder may be solely responsible for the maintenance of the properties (this is normally reflected in the level of the rent), or may agree to undertake repairs (usually charging back to the leaseholder). In other cases the leaseholder may be responsible for carrying out any necessary repairs to the satisfaction of the freeholder.

It is unwise to invest a lot of money in converting or refurbishing a leasehold which is subject to regular rent reviews, especially in low rental city centre areas. The arts tend to act as a catalyst for new activities and once an area begins to show signs of revitalisation, the rents increase. Small galleries used to flourish in London's Covent Garden, then they moved to dockland warehouses; both these areas are now considered to be far too expensive.

The lease of properties can be sold but in certain situations the agreement between the freeholder and the initial leaseholder remains in force.

Where any form of leasehold agreement is being considered, the advice of an experienced solicitor should be sought.

BUYING THE FREEHOLD
Acquiring a property freehold means the purchaser owns both the property and the land on which it is built in perpetuity. The only controls on what is built on the site, what changes are made to the original building and what activities take place in the buildings are those imposed by legislation (i.e. planning, building controls, licensing laws etc.).

VALUING THE PROPERTY
The value of a property cannot be defined as a simple figure. When a property is changing hands, the value is however much a potential purchaser is prepared to pay.

The value of a site or building in commercial terms is based on the income it could produce. In this sense, many arts buildings have a negative value in that they cost more to run than they produce in income, giving a negative return on the capital investment. An existing warehouse or redundant school may therefore be more valuable in commercial terms in its original state (given that the structure is sound) than it is after several hundred thousands pounds has been spent in converting it for arts use.

Buildings which have been used as theatres (whether designed for that purpose or converted from some other use) are protected by legislation as planning permission has to be sought for change of use. The main value of a theatre building, in commercial terms, could lie in the potential value of the land which it occupies. It is unlikely that 'change of use' permission would be granted while the theatre is well used. This means that an arts building which is operating successfully can be valued at less than one which is falling into disuse.

This hypothetical commercial value of arts buildings is relevant if some form of mortgage is being considered in which the building is offered as security. It also affects the financial calculations which a developer would make in considering including provision for the arts in a new building complex.

INSURING THE PROPERTY
It is important to arrange for the building to be covered by insurance immediately it passes into the ownership of the purchaser. It should be insured for its replacement value. This is not the same as the purchase price. (Replacement value covers design and building costs at current prices but excludes the cost of the land.)

A building which is in a poor state of repair presents a potential hazard. Where it is adjacent to a public route, passers-by could be injured or their vehicles damaged if any part of the structure were to fall on them. Anyone visiting a building (e.g. someone asked to inspect the building, or who represents the owners) could suffer injury if, for instance, rotten flooring or staircases were to give way. In English law, people injured in this way have to prove negligence on the part of the owner before they receive compensation; in order to avoid long drawn out court cases and as a matter of responsible ownership, it is advisable to take out 'accident cover' to insure against such eventualities.

CHECKS TO BE MADE ON THE SITE

SIZE
A site obviously needs to be large enough to accommodate the building which is to be built on it. In addition to the space required by the actual building, areas are needed for access, delivery and parking. If there is any doubt that the facilities can be fitted on the site, an architect should be commissioned to carry out a feasibility study.

DESIGNATION OF THE AREA
This is shown in the structure plan drawn up by the local authority. The position of the site on that plan has an affect on the likelihood of planning permission being granted. It also gives an indication of how the area is likely to develop in the future. For instance, an attractive old warehouse surrounded by a mix of buildings, may be located in the centre of an area designated for industrial development. This would be detrimental to its long-term future use as an arts facility. On the other hand, such a building could also be situated in a conservation area. This would help retain the overall character of the surroundings, but could limit the scope for the conversion of the property and inhibit its development as an arts facility.

FUTURE DEVELOPMENTS
Checks should be made for any proposed development in the area (these could have either a beneficial or a detrimental effect), such as new roads and road improvements, housing redevelopments, etc. The local authority planning staff

should be able to advise on what proposals there are for the area.

CONDITION OF THE SITE

In certain situations it may be advisable to check the previous uses of the site and the condition of the subsoil. In urban areas with a long history of development, some sites are in a condition which makes them expensive to build on. They may be left with pollutants following years of industrial use or the crumbling foundations of several layers of old buildings. In extreme cases, the previous use may inhibit development or cause long delays while the problems are sorted out. (Burial grounds, for instance, can only be built on after certain procedures have been formally completed.)

VEHICULAR ACCESS

Large and medium scale performance-based buildings and galleries are often handling very bulky material. Vehicles transporting equipment and exhibition material need to be able to get to an arts building easily and to deliver the goods to the right part of the building. Low bridges and narrow roads 'en route' to the site present problems for pantechnicons.

ACCESS ROADS

Where the site or building is not on a public road, checks should be made to ensure that access will be maintained or provided. The status of any non-public authority feeder roads needs to be established, along with who owns them and how they are maintained.

CAR PARKING FACILITIES

Arts buildings can generate heavy traffic and require a substantial amount of parking spaces. Both traffic regulations and car parking requirements should be checked with the local authority. In some situations, car parking provision may only need to be made for staff and special user groups. In others, a large number of cars may have to be accommodated on the site - in urban areas, many local authorities will not give planning permission to uses which generate additional on-street parking.

SERVICES

Checks should be made to ensure that all the normal services are available or can be supplied (e.g. electricity, gas, water, sewage disposal, telephones, etc.).

CHECKS TO BE MADE ON THE BUILDING

Where a building is being considered some additional checks need to be carried out.

STRUCTURAL CONDITION

The state of the roof, guttering and downpipes, pointing, window and door frames, will give some indication of whether a major refurbishment or a 'patch and paint' job is required.

Whatever the apparent state of the building, a full structural survey should be carried out by a professionally qualified person before any steps are taken towards acquiring the building. The survey will give more information about the likely costs and the scale of what needs to be done. When major structural alterations are being considered it is important to check which parts of the building are load bearing and whether they are capable of carrying more weight without further strengthening.

SCOPE FOR CONVERSION

Before starting to search for a suitable building, it is advisable to make a list of the main requirements, based on the proposed uses. Spaces need to be described in terms of their dimensions (length, breadth and height), their position and relationship to one another (e.g. accessible from exterior, or ground floor position), their character (e.g. good natural daylight, or long blank wall space) and the number needed.

It is important to consider changes of level and access routes both in terms of whether the building can be made accessible to all its users (artists and staff as well as members of the audience) and whether the necessary equipment can be got into the building and moved around easily. Frequent changes of level, narrow staircases, doors and corridors present problems.

Where a building occupies the whole of its site, the essential space requirements must be met within the existing structure. Where additional vacant land is available on the site, it is worth considering whether some activities could be accommodated by building an addition or extension.

RESTRICTIONS ON USE

It is also worth checking whether there are any restrictions on the use to which a building can be put. These could be contained in some form of deed or covenant. Religious and educational buildings, where they were originally provided by an individual benefactor or charitable group, may have restrictions on gambling or sale of alcohol or even dramatic performances.

FINANCE AND FUNDING

This chapter looks at the financial aspects of building for the arts. The main headings are as follows:

FINANCING THE ARTS
which outlines the main sources of arts funding.

FINANCIAL PROCEDURES
which covers cash flow planning, fundraising and arranging loans and mortgages.

COSTS
which gives guidance on how to work out the costs involved in a building project.

SOURCES OF FUNDING
which lists the main sources of grants for capital projects.

FINANCING THE ARTS

There are a number of sources of finance for the arts and a range of organisations involved in their funding. Government spending on the arts is, in the main, channelled through a number of non-governmental organisations. The largest of these is the Arts Council, with its budget of £174 million (1990-91). Some of this money is directed to the Scottish and Welsh Arts Councils and to the Regional Arts Associations in England. The British Film Institute, the Crafts Council and the Museums and Galleries Commission are also concerned with the financing of arts activities. They are funded separately by the Office of Arts and Libraries.

Most of the money is spent in promoting the arts, on subsidising arts productions, and on supporting arts projects. A very small percentage is made available for capital projects.

The second partner in the funding triangle is local government. A major provider of buildings, it has also been increasing its level of revenue support to arts organisations in recent years and now contributes a greater proportion than do the central arts bodies. It does this in three ways. A wide range of facilities are run directly by local authorities. Many other arts venues and companies receive regular grants on an annual basis to support their work. In addition, the Regional Arts Associations are partially funded by the local authorities within their areas.

The ability of local government to raise and spend money, however, is becoming increasingly limited. Where capital projects are being planned, local government is increasingly looking to planning agreements to help off-set some of the costs. (See the chapter on 'Planning Gain and Development Opportunities' later in this section.)

The third partner is the private sector. A substantial proportion of the money to pay artists and mount arts activities has always been earned income i.e. ticket sales, fees, sales of works, books, records, etc. This has been supplemented by other earnings - catering facilities, shops, lettings - and by donations. Traditionally, the arts have also benefited from a generous input of time and skills from the general public. However, the private sector is now being seen as a major source of funding. With 'challenge funding' money provided by the government (channelled through the Association for Business Sponsorship of the Arts), tax concessions for corporations and individuals who give to the arts, and the Arts Council's Incentive Funding Scheme, the private sector is being encouraged to provide sufficient extra money to compensate for the financial stringencies within which the other two members have to operate. Its contribution through business sponsorship in 1989 was estimated as being about £30 million.

Any organisation considering building needs to be aware of the changing financial situation, its limitations and its opportunities, and operate within it.

FINANCIAL PROCEDURES
CASH FLOW PLANNING
A building project can only be brought to a satisfactory completion if there is sufficient money available to cover the costs. This is not just a matter of the total income being equal to the total expenditure though this has to be seen as a prerequisite. It is also necessary to ensure that sufficient cash is available to meet the costs on a month by month basis.

A building project can extend over several years from its inception to its completion. Some expenditure will be fairly evenly spread over the whole period (e.g. the administrative costs) while other expenditure requires large sums to be available at particular times. Cash flow planning is required to ensure that money is available when it is needed.

Where money is being raised from outside sources, there are a number of factors which contribute to delays between the money being raised and its being available for spending. For example, some funding bodies make their grants payable against evidence of the work having been completed, others promise funding in future years. Where donations are covenanted, payments are normally made over a four year period. To get the full amount due, tax has to be reclaimed annually.

It is advisable to make detailed charts showing anticipated income and expenditure on a month by month basis. Some organisations may find it helpful to divide the cash flow charts into a series of 'work phases' as outlined below. Cost projections can also be analysed under a series of 'heads of expenditure' as listed in the paragraphs on 'Costs' at the end of this chapter.

DIVIDING THE PROJECT INTO PHASES OF WORK
There are four main phases of work involved in the administration of a capital project. These relate to:
- the initial research and planning;

- the development of the project to outline design stage;

- the detailed design;

- the construction of the building.

During each of these stages some financial commitment is incurred. The amounts of money involved increase substantially as the project progresses with the greatest expenditure being incurred in the final stage - the construction of the building. At the end of each phase, cash flow projections need to be reviewed and a decision made as to whether the project can go ahead as planned or whether amendments need to be made.

PLANNING THE FINANCE TO COVER CONSTRUCTION COSTS
The bulk of the expenditure is incurred once the construction work starts. These costs have to be met as the project progresses. (See the chapter in Section 1 on 'The Building Process'.)

As the project develops, the cash flow projections

need to be kept under review and amended to take account of changes in the building programme, increases in costs and fluctuations in anticipated income levels. Properly prepared cash flow projections enable any shortfall to be anticipated and demonstrate to potential sources of bridging finance how the loan is to be repaid. Discussions about bridging finance need to be held well before the contract is let so that the necessary finance is assured to enable the project to proceed smoothly through to completion.

Where the bridging finance is raised through normal commercial sources, interest has to be paid in line with the prevailing rates. This interest requirement then has to be put into the cash flow projections and the total fundraising sum adjusted accordingly. It is obviously advantageous to get money in as quickly as possible. Any available money which is surplus to immediate requirements can then be invested so that the interest is added to the total amount raised. This will help offset the interest which has to be paid while the project is in shortfall. Where a large proportion of the potential income is in the form of covenants, the cash flow projections are likely to move in and out of shortfall on a regular basis.

FUNDRAISING

For many arts organisations the only way of financing a building project is to mount a public appeal. Many such appeals have achieved their targets in the past and some have been very successful in raising the necessary money in a comparatively short time. There is no one key element to a successful appeal. Inevitably, luck plays a part but careful planning, a realistic budget, and a well worked out strategy are all strong contributory factors.

The appeal needs to be planned well in advance, but should not be launched until its viability can be established. When the appeal is launched, those being approached for funds will want clear and substantiated information about the promoting organisation, what the project involves, the timescale, the budget, how the money is to be raised, what controls there are over expenditure and what money is available to run the completed facility. It is also useful to be able to give people an indication of how the completed building will look.

A realistic target figure needs to be established and potential sources of funding identified at an early stage. The total sum which has to be raised needs to be broken down into smaller target sums. These may relate to possible funding sources (i.e. a certain amount from the local authorities and a certain amount from major industries in the area) or may relate to specific elements of the building (e.g. so much towards the educational facilities, or to provide for people with disabilities). It may also be worth considering linking large donations to easily identifiable sections of the building and naming them after the donor (e.g. The XXX Gallery, or The XXX Cafe). It is advisable to do some research on the amount of money the organisations being approached have given in the past in order to make realistic estimates and requests. Increasingly, trusts and companies are developing closely defined policies for their charitable giving so research should be carried out so that approaches can be targeted effectively. There are publications which give this information. (See bibliography.)

The recommended technique is to identify the major potential givers and earmark a sum to be raised from each. This usually starts with the larger sums and works down. If one or two such potential givers can be drawn into the project at an early stage (e.g. as members of the co-ordinating committee), and are prepared to make the initial commitments, they could help establish the level for other donations. Fundraisers advise that smaller sums should not be accepted from organisations targeted for major donations until a sufficient number of the larger sums is committed. Appeals tend to be run on the pyramid basis. For instance, it might be decided to try to raise 50% of the total sum from a relatively small number of organisations. The next 30% might be raised from a larger number of smaller organisations, leaving the remaining 20% to come from a general public appeal.

The whole process has to be co-ordinated and conducted on a methodical basis. Even though a large number of people may be involved in sending out letters, making telephone calls and following up contacts, the timing, presentation of information, amounts to be asked for, etc. are best controlled by one responsible individual or a small co-ordinating group.

Systems for processing the money and for obtaining the maximum tax benefits need to be set up. The publicity material should explain how donations can be made, what the advantages are of the different types of giving, and provide those being approached with the necessary documents to make the gift. Special forms, drawn up in accordance with current legislation and explaining the tax advantages of a covenanted donation, should be made available to all potential donors. These are known as 'Deeds of Covenant' or as 'Bonds of Annuity' (in Scotland). The legislation covering sponsorship and charitable giving changes fairly regularly so it is advisable to take specialist advice or obtain up to date information from the available published sources.

The presentation of the project is important. Organisations which have a record of charitable giving tend to be inundated with requests and proposals. Long and insistent telephone calls are not a recommended method of approach. Meetings are best arranged through mutual contacts, armed with publicity material setting out the basic facts of the organisation and the proposed project as succinctly as possible. If a meeting can be arranged, a quick and potentially effective way of getting a message across is through the use of video. Here the arts are at an advantage, as they have both a visual appeal and people with the necessary presentation skills.

It is normal for a fundraising programme to

continue throughout the construction period. This is acceptable provided it is recognised that the amount of funds raised over a period tends to follow a standard pattern. This starts low, increases fairly rapidly, peaks and then starts its downward slide. Apart from one or two minor peaks coinciding with publicity linked to highlights in the building process, the pattern of diminishing returns is a fixed one.

LOANS AND MORTGAGES

Arts organisations need their revenue income (and any additional money they can raise) to cover their running costs, so it is unlikely that there will be any surplus available to repay outstanding debts. In general, loans should only be regarded as an advance of anticipated income and not as a major part of the funding package.

There are occasions when a loan can be a useful tool in holding the financial package together. For instance, it may be necessary to purchase or lease a building or site at short notice to prevent it going to another buyer. In other cases, a loan facility might be used to underwrite the project or bridge a gap between the promise of funding and the payment of the grant. Loans can also be raised against projected covenant income to enable a building project to go ahead.

There are also some situations where a capital investment is directly linked to an increase in revenue income, where some form of loan facility could be considered. A brewery, for instance, might offer a loan to fund a bar and catering facilities secured against future bar sales. An organisation might consider taking on a loan to increase the seating capacity of its existing building, with a view to repaying the money out of the additional income raised.

Arts buildings tend not to be an appropriate form for raising mortgages. If a building is acquired for conversion, a mortgage could be considered to cover the purchase of the building but it is unlikely that mortgage finance could help towards the improvement costs. (See chapter on 'Site and Buildings' under the heading 'Valuing the Property'.) In general, a mortgage is only appropriate if it is seen as an alternative to paying rent for a building which does not need substantial alteration.

Loans to bridge the gap between immediate expenditure and anticipated income normally need to be negotiated through a bank. Occasionally a sympathetic local authority can help with a loan at an advantageous rate of interest or interest-free, the interest being seen as a form of grant. Some commercial companies might consider providing some sort of bridging finance as their contribution to a project, rather than making a direct donation.

COSTS

Cost projections need to be worked out at an early stage and kept under review as decisions are made and the project progresses.

Information on the costs which are likely to be incurred during the building project is set out below under main heads of expenditure. These are:

Administration
Consultants
Publicity and public relations
Fundraising
Financing the project (loans and guarantees)
Site and/or building acquisition
Design work
Construction work
Fitting out (furnishings, fittings and equipment)

ADMINISTRATION

There is a need to spend money on administration at every stage in the project.

A full-time co-ordinator is required for all but the smallest projects. During the early stages, the co-ordinator carries out, or co-ordinates the initial planning, the feasibility and development studies and the writing of the brief. He/she works with the design team on the design development. Once the contractor is on site, the co-ordinator has to oversee the finance, sort out problems and take decisions as necessary to ensure the work progresses. Time is also required to continue fund raising, programme planning, appointing staff, booking in events etc. In a large project, or where most of the detailed work is being undertaken in house, a team of people may be needed.

Some money is required to meet incidental costs: travel for seminars, training sessions, conferences; tickets for arts events; publications; membership or affiliation subscriptions to useful organisation; fees for planning applications, registration as a company, etc.

Most of this expenditure is incurred during the first phase of the project.

CONSULTANCY COSTS

Very few organisations have all the necessary expertise which is required to plan and develop an arts building. Arts organisations are likely to need specialist help with financial and building-related matters. Non-arts organisation may have expertise in these areas but may lack the specialist knowledge required to plan the use, programming, management, staffing and funding of the facility as well as to brief the design team on the spaces, layout and equipment needed.

The bulk of the cost of this consultancy work is incurred during the first stage. The amount of time required varies with the nature and complexity of the project and the expertise already available within the initiating organisation.

The costs of the consultants commissioned to design the building come under 'design costs'.

PUBLICITY AND PUBLIC RELATIONS

Where a promotional campaign is needed to build up and retain support, some expenditure is incurred. Costs may include publicising and holding meetings, hiring premises, writing, designing and producing publicity material, and paying for professional advice.

The costs of promotion and publicity will continue throughout the project, with peak expenditure periods when the initial support is being built up and again towards the end of the building stage.

FUNDRAISING

Where the costs, in whole or in part, have to be met through fundraising, the campaign needs to be planned while the proposals are being tested and developed. Expenditure is incurred in paying for the time spent in researching and planning the campaign, in making applications and approaches and in preparing and producing the necessary support material.

The cost of launching the campaign comes at the beginning of the second phase - the briefing and initial design phase. The large part of the costs of running the campaign also have to be met during this second phase as there needs to be a clear indication that the money can be raised before the architect is commissioned to prepare detailed designs. The costs of running the campaign continue throughout the building process and possibly after the building is opened.

PAYING FOR BRIDGING FINANCE

Projects which are dependent on grants and fundraising to cover the capital costs are likely to require some form of loan or guarantee facility to ensure that money is available as it is required. This represents an additional cost to be taken into account.

SITE OR BUILDING ACQUISITION

The first major expense is likely to be the acquisition of a site or building. Where land or an existing building has to be bought outright a considerable outlay is required. Certain leasehold arrangements can reduce the amount of money which needs to be found at the outset but these normally involve an annual rental. It may be possible to find an organisation which is willing to buy the land and then lease it back for the arts use. (Local authorities are empowered to acquire land for purposes which are deemed to benefit the community.)

It is better to avoid launching an appeal for the purchase money which is separate from the major appeal. If it is not possible to delay the purchase until the plans can be worked out in sufficient detail to launch the main appeal, some form of loan facility could be considered.

DESIGN WORK

Once a project is underway (i.e. at the 'initial design' stage) the design fees are related to the building costs on a percentage basis. Until then, the appropriate design consultants are commissioned as required and are paid on a time basis. The size and composition of the team of people appointed to work on the design varies with the size and complexity of the building.

(See the chapters in Section 1 on ' The Design Process' and in Section 2 on 'Working with Consultants'.)

THE CONSTRUCTION COSTS

As the cost of the building work (and related fees) usually holds the key to whether or not a project goes ahead, it is advisable to get some idea of the likely cost at a very early stage. More accurate estimates can be made as the project progresses.

EARLY GUESSES

The first way to get some idea of the cost involved is to make comparisons with other buildings. It is unlikely that any organisation will want to reproduce a facility built elsewhere, so a reasonably comparable building (or parts of a building) needs to be identified on which costs comparisons can be based. In making such comparisons, inflation has to be taken into account. Inflation in the building industry does not necessarily follow the standard patterns. It goes up steeply in times of a construction boom, and stays stationary in times of a building slump. Building costs also vary according to the part of the country the project is in.

INITIAL ESTIMATES

Some initial design work is needed to get a more reliable figure. This may involve working out the volume of the main spaces and making an assessment of the amount of ancillary space required. If this is done, the costs can then be calculated on a 'cost per square metre basis', in line with current building costs for comparable spaces. The specialist sections of the building (e.g. stage and auditorium) may need to be worked out in greater detail and the 'cost per square metre' will be substantially higher than for the less specialised areas.

When an existing building is being considered for conversion to arts use, two separate aspects affect the cost. Firstly the building has to be brought into a reasonable state of structural repair. (It may be necessary to undertake this work as soon as the building is acquired in order to prevent further deterioration to the fabric.) Secondly, the building has to be made suitable for the proposed arts use. A surveyor or building contractor will give a fairly reliable estimate of the cost of the initial repair work. The conversion and fitting out costs can only be calculated once the uses have been determined and an outline design prepared.

Estimates which are made without any initial design work being undertaken can only give a very broad indication of the likely costs.

ESTIMATES BASED ON THE ARCHITECT'S DESIGN

Once the initial design work has been done, the scheme can be costed by a quantity surveyor. The more detailed the design, the more reliable the estimates will be. They should, however, still be regarded as indicative at this stage.

THE BUILDING CONTRACTOR'S PRICE FOR THE WORK

The prices received from the building contractors give the first practical indication of what the project will cost. These may relate closely to the quantity surveyor's estimates or may vary quite considerably.

The tender price is not necessarily the end price for the job. Once the building work has been completed the final account has to be settled. This final figure includes a number of additional sums.

(See the chapter in Section 1 on ' The Building Process'.)

FITTING OUT THE BUILDING
The costs of equipping and fitting out an arts building are far more substantial than many people realise. (In a new building, they can they can account for as much as 40% of the total construction cost.)

Where specialist provision is required, separate specifications may be drawn up and costed. This work is normally undertaken by a theatre consultant.

For small conversion jobs where a builder is carrying out the structural work only, provision has to be made for fitting out the building shell. Some agreements with developers also provide a building shell to be fitting out by the users.

(See the chapter in Section 2 on 'Planning Gain and Development Opportunities'.)

SOURCES OF FUNDING
Many new facilities for the arts are financed from a number of different sources, with a 'funding package' being built up to cover the capital costs. Most of these packages rely on a substantial input from a local authority - as direct provision from its own resources, through use of EC or government programmes, or through negotiations with developers.

When formal approaches are made to the various funding bodies it is helpful if they can be given some indication of how the total funding package is to be put together. Funding bodies have limited resources and prefer to commit money to schemes which are likely to go ahead. It is an advantage, therefore, if some money is already secured when the approach is made. This also applies to appeals directed towards the public or towards the private sector.

The Arts Council has commissioned a series of case studies to demonstrate how arts organisations have been able to draw on various sources of funding. These will be published, together with information on sources of funding, later this year (1990).

MONEY FROM EUROPE
Grants made by the EC towards the cost of providing facilities for the arts are made through the European Regional Development Fund. They have, in the past, been linked to the increased employment opportunities which the new developments were to provide. For example, theatres at Pitlochry in Scotland and at Plymouth in Devon received substantial grants on the basis that the areas they served were dependent on the tourist industry, which would benefit from new arts provision.

The European Funds are undergoing a major review and it is likely that funding will be more sharply focussed in the future on areas of special need. The Arts Council's publication 'Who Does What in Europe' provides a comprehensive guide to EC organisations.

CENTRAL GOVERNMENT SOURCES
There are no funds available from central government sources which are specifically directed towards the provision of arts facilities, nor even towards the more general improvement of opportunities for recreation.

At any one time, there may be a number of government operated schemes from which funding can be obtained, but it is necessary to study their terms of provision carefully. Listed below are some of the schemes which have provided capital finance for the arts in the past and which are still operating along the same lines. More detailed information can be obtained from the publication 'Government Grants - A Guide for Voluntary Organisation', written by Maggie Jones and published by the National Council for Voluntary Organisations. It is now in its fifth edition and is updated on a regular basis.

THE URBAN PROGRAMME
The Department of the Environment (DoE) provides money through its Urban Programme to enable local government to deal with economic, social and environmental problems through innovative projects. The DoE provides 75% of the cost of approved schemes with the remaining 25% coming from the local authority's own funds.

There are fifty-seven local authorities in England in receipt of Urban Programme funds. These include: Birmingham, Gateshead, Hackney, Islington, Lambeth, Liverpool, Manchester, Newcastle and Salford. Information on current programme authorities can be obtained from the Department of the Environment.

CONSERVATION AND HISTORIC BUILDINGS
Formerly the responsibility of the DoE, historic buildings now fall within the orbit of the Historic Buildings and Monuments Commission for England (more commonly known as English Heritage).

English Heritage gives grants towards the cost of repairing buildings 'of outstanding historic or architectural interest in national terms' and buildings which make a significant contribution to the character of a conservation area.

In the main, the grants are only offered to help towards the cost of putting the building into a good state of structural repair. Most of them relate to the exterior of the building.

DEPARTMENT OF EDUCATION AND SCIENCE
Some arts buildings might qualify for capital grants relating to the provision of facilities for young people.

SCOTTISH OFFICE AND WELSH OFFICE
Information on government grant schemes in

Scotland and Wales (where they are not covered by the schemes outlined above) can be obtained through the Scottish and Welsh Offices.

ORGANISATIONS FINANCED BY THE GOVERNMENT

ARTS COUNCIL

The Arts Council currently offers grants towards feasibility studies for new buildings and improvements to existing buildings. It is also introducing some capital provision in 1991-92 as part of its Incentive Funding Scheme. The Arts Council's Housing the Arts fund was brought to a close in 1985.

BRITISH FILM INSTITUTE

Applications for capital grants now fall within the terms of reference of the recently introduced Development Budget. This is an 'incentive' scheme which means that grants are given on the basis of 2:1 (private funding/new earned income:grant). This scheme replaced the Housing the Cinema Fund in 1988.

COMMISSION FOR RACIAL EQUALITY

The Commission is able to fund projects which promote equal opportunities or create racial harmony. Some capital funds are offered towards the cost of providing facilities within a building but no money is available towards the cost of purchasing land or property.

CRAFTS COUNCIL

The Council makes occasional small grants, particularly towards the cost of upgrading existing facilities. Any grant has to be heavily matched and only projects of national significance can be considered.

MUSEUMS AND GALLERIES COMMISSION

The Commission administers an annual grant scheme which aims to help English non-national museums meet the cost of the construction work required to create additional or improved accommodation for museum collections and/or related conservation facilities.

RURAL DEVELOPMENT COMMISSION

The Development Commission is concerned with the alleviation of social and economic problems in rural areas of England. Capital grants are available under two headings:

Village Halls. Grants can be made towards the costs of converting or making improvements to existing village halls so they can accommodate new activities, and also towards the cost of the purchase and adaptation of redundant buildings to provide community facilities where none exist.

Local Enterprise Agencies. Rural Project Grants provide capital funding to help set up and develop small rural businesses. (Print and craft workshops may be regarded as small businesses.)

SPORTS COUNCIL

The Sports Council provides capital grants and interest-free loans for the provision of local sports facilities. Such facilities could be designed to make provision for some arts uses. Dance activities fall partly within the Sports Council's area of interest.

Funding is also available to help projects of a wider than local significance in areas which were previously eligible for support from the Greater London Council or the Metropolitan County Councils.

LOCAL AUTHORITIES

Local Authorities are empowered to make grants for a whole range of activities which can be held to benefit the local community. There are a number of tiers within the local government structure, any of which could have funding provision:

- County Authorities

- District (Borough or City) Councils

- Town or Parish Councils

- Local Education Authorities

County and District Councils have concurrent powers in respect of the support of the arts and it is always worth approaching both. The level of response will vary with the policies and interests of the particular authority and the nature and scope of the individual project.

After the abolition of the Greater London Council the London Boroughs got together to form the London Boroughs Grants Scheme to look after the interests of the numerous voluntary organisations which had depended on GLC funding. This body is not able to offer capital funding - any funding which is available comes from the individual boroughs.

The main point of contact for arts organisations is with the Departments of Recreation and Leisure Services but there may also be links with Education Departments as well as those concerned with community and social issues. A local authority has the power to acquire land or buildings for any of their functions or for the benefit, improvement or development of their area.

Local authorities also administer a grant scheme for conservation projects (Town Scheme Grants) and some will offer funds towards the cost of preserving historic buildings.

Some of the government's urban development initiatives are funded in co-operation with local authorities.

CHARITABLE TRUSTS

There are many thousand trusts throughout the country, distributing some £250 million in total each year. Each of them operates within the terms of its foundation. Many of them are small, locally-based and dealing with single issues. Only a proportion are enabled to make capital grants. Some may only make donations to registered charities. The trusts give money in response to applications for projects which fall within their terms of reference. Any organisation applying for grants has, therefore, to work through the

available directories making lists of possible
sources of funding on the basis of geographical
location, aims of organisation, services provided,
etc.

There are a number of directories which provide
this information. Some public libraries also draw
up lists of trusts which relate specifically to their
own areas. The main publications are:

Directory of Grant Making Trusts. Published
every second year, this lists some 2,500 trusts
each with an annual income in excess of £1,500.

Guide to the Major Trusts. Published every
second year, this gives more detailed information
on 240 grant-making trusts which donate in
excess of £90,000 a year.

Further details are given in the bibliography.

CARNEGIE UK TRUST
The Carnegie UK Trust launched a scheme in
1989 offering capital challenge grants towards the
cost of making arts venues more accessible to
people with disabilities. The scheme is called
ADAPT (Access for Disabled People to Arts
Premises Today) and grants are available for new
buildings and improving existing buildings.

BUSINESS AND INDUSTRY
Of the estimated £30 million which business and
industry gave to the arts in 1989, most was in the
form of sponsorship. Due in some part to the way
the tax legislation operates, very little sponsorship money goes towards the cost of capital
projects. Some direct grants are made towards
appeals by local industrial and commercial
organisations and some major companies have
contributed to the building appeals of the national
companies.

Advice is available from the Association for
Business Sponsorship of the Arts which provides
a link between sponsors and projects seeking
sponsorship. It also operates the Business
Sponsorship Incentive Scheme which adds
government money to that provided by business
and industry in new sponsorship projects.

PLANNING GAIN AND DEVELOP-
MENT OPPORTUNITIES

This chapter collects together information
relating to incorporating arts provision into new
developments.

It is divided into three parts:

ARTS PROVISION IN NEW
DEVELOPMENTS
which looks at the scope for arts provision, where
the initiative comes from how opportunities for
'planning gain' arise and the increasing use of
'planning agreements'.

WORKING WITH DEVELOPERS
which looks at the types of offers made and how
these can be best used by arts organisations.

ARTS ORGANISATIONS AS DEVELOPERS
which looks at how arts organisations can take
the initiative in developing their own properties.

ARTS PROVISION IN NEW
DEVELOPMENTS
Increasing attention is being given to the role of
the arts within the communities they serve. The
experiences of cities such as Bradford, Glasgow,
Liverpool, Sheffield, Southampton, and Swansea
demonstrates how arts-related projects can help
to revitalise an area.

The Arts Council's publication 'An Urban Renaissance - sixteen case studies showing the role of
the arts in urban regeneration' illustrates what
can be achieved.

INITIATIVES FOR NEW DEVELOPMENTS
The initiative for introducing arts provision into a
new development can come from a number of
sources:

- Development Corporations

- Local Authorities

- Commercial developers

- Other interested groups

*DEVELOPMENT CORPORATIONS AND LOCAL
AUTHORITIES*
The public development corporations and local
authorities, in areas of urban deprivation, are still
able to draw on funds for capital projects. New
arts projects are being used as catalysts for urban
renewal. Public funds are invested in a new or
refurbished arts building with the aim of providing a focal point for regeneration which will draw
private money into improving the surrounding
area. There are a number of examples of arts
projects which have made a contribution to the
regeration of urban areas - in inner cities, dock-
lands, and old industrial sites.

Local authorities can also use the powers they
have through the planning legislation to negotiate
benefits for the local community when they are
disposing of land which they own or when
planning permission is being sought. (See
'Planning Gain and Planning Agreements' below.)

DEVELOPERS
Developers may also have an interest in including
some provision for the arts in a new scheme. This
may be in response to a planning requirement for
a mixed development or an initiative on the part
of the developer to get support for the overall
scheme. In large scale developments, the inclusion of an arts facility can increase the market
value of the commercial and residential properties in that it:

- attracts people to the area, increasing the potential profitability of the shops, restaurants,
  and related service industries;

- extends the time people spend in an area by
  introducing an evening and weekend use;

- gives identity to a new area which might otherwise be an anonymous collection of commercial spaces;

- provides facilities for the people who are to work in the offices, shops, etc.

OTHER GROUPS
The role of groups other than the public authorities and the private developers is limited unless they happen to own land which is integral to a development proposal.

PLANNING AGREEMENTS AND PLANNING GAIN
With local authority expenditure continuing to be tightly controlled, direct provision of arts facilities is becoming increasingly difficult. Local authorities are therefore looking for other ways of funding community facilities. The main method of stimulating the funding of such facilities by the private sector is through the use of the planning powers.

PLANNING GAIN
Planning gain relates to a concept of benefit accruing to the community from the commercial development of land in that community. The potential for 'planning gain' arises when there is a strong market demand for a particular use and a limited supply of sites. It often involves a change of use which substantially enhances the value of the land (e.g. the redevelopment of open space or of an existing public building for commercial purposes), the relaxation of normal planning requirements (e.g. increased density), or some departure from the local plan (e.g. to build office space in an area which is designated for other uses). It can also arise when a proposed development has a direct effect on an existing facility (e.g. the demolition of a public building containing a hall). In such cases, the granting of planning permission may be linked to new or additional community facilities being provided or financed.

THE INCREASING USE OF NEGOTIATED AGREEMENTS
Because of the way the planning laws were used by some authorities in the past, the term 'planning gain' carries with it some connotations of the imposition of a levy on development. In the current political and economic climate, the trend is towards negotiated solutions or 'planning agreements' (sometimes referred to as 'Section 52 agreements'). The effect is to move away from direct cash payments, particularly where they are used to contribute to a community use which is not directly linked to the area being redeveloped, towards agreeing the development mix of commercial and community uses. A negotiated solution, or planning agreement, is worked out between the local authority and the developer to provide a balanced development on terms which are acceptable to both parties. The amount of 'community benefit' which can be included in any development is directly related to the potential margin of profit to be made on the commercial sections. Where arts provision is being considered, the 'value enhancement' factor also needs to be taken into consideration.

The principal provisions concerning planning agreements are found in section 52 of the 1971 Town and Country Planning Act, and permit the authority to enter into agreements which permanently or temporarily restrict or regulate the development or use of land within the authority's area. Furthermore, they may contain such 'incidental or consequential provisions (including provisions of a financial nature) as appear to the local planning authority to be necessary or expedient for the purpose of the agreement'.

The above definition is taken from the publication 'Planning Gain' published by the organisation Planning Aid for London. It gives a detailed analysis of the subject and is written with the aim of helping community groups to understand how planning agreements operate and how they can take advantage of the opportunities offered.

Examples of arts projects which have been financed through some form of planning agreement are included in Appendix 1.

LOOKING OUT FOR OPPORTUNITIES
Planning agreements are negotiated between local authorities and private developers. If arts organisations are to take advantage of opportunities which may be available, they need to:

- be aware of what is happening in the local property market and make their interest known at an early stage;

- have outline plans for a new facility or improvements to their existing building which demonstrate what can be done should money or help become available;

- build up good working relationships with local authority officers and local councillors so that their needs are known and their interests represented;

- make contact with developers who are known to have an interest in the area;

- familiarise themselves with the criteria for development in their area and get some understanding of the financial stakes.

WORKING WITH DEVELOPERS
Planning gain agreements can offer a number of different opportunities for arts centres to improve their existing buildings or relocate to new premises.

The opportunities which arise are likely to be presented in one of the following ways.

A LUMP SUM PAYMENT OR CASH CONTRIBUTION TOWARDS A CAPITAL PROJECT
These are becoming less common, though may be made where a new development has a direct impact on an existing building or impinges on its site. For example:

- The Everyman Theatre, Cheltenham, was helped to rebuild the whole of its backstage area when a large shopping centre was built immediately adjacent to the old structure;

- The Phoenix Arts Centre, Leicester, was helped to relocate its entrance and extend and improve its foyer area to enable a proposed building to use the whole of the adjacent site.

A NEW FACILITY

Large scale developments present opportunities for new arts provision to be included to provide a mixed development and/or enhance the value of the commercial section. For example:

- the Barbican Centre provided a focus of interest and activity in a major new development;

- a redundant dockland warehouse was converted to house the Tate Gallery Liverpool as part of a policy to regenerate the surrounding redundant dockland area.

Note: Both projects were financed by public funds.

A FACILITY WITHIN A NEW BUILDING OR COMPLEX

This could take the form of a 'shell' being provided which the arts organisation fits out and furnishes for its own use. For example:

- Windsor Community Arts Centre was provided with accommodation in a refurbished court house as part of an agreement giving permission for office development for the rest of the building;

- Richmond Orange Tree Theatre is being re-housed as part of a planning agreement permitting commercial development on the site of a redundant school building;

- Epsom, Surrey was provided with a new small theatre space when a town centre development led to the demolition of the existing public hall.

A SHARED FACILITY

Where a commercial exhibition space, entertainment facility or conference hall is provided, a local authority might negotiate a certain amount of time to be dedicated to reserved uses such as the promotion of a programme of concerts or touring art exhibitions.

In all but the first option, the responsibility for the design and planning of the project lies primarily with the developer, not the arts organisation. While many developers employ highly skilled teams of designers, their specialisation lies in commercial development and their brief will be to maximise the potential return on investment.

If the arts provision is to operate successfully, some specialists arts design input is required at an early stage. In many cases, this is best achieved by a consultant designer working with the developer's design team to advise on the requirements for the arts provision. The developer may agree that it is in his/her best interests and make such an appointment. In other cases, the arts organisation may have to be prepared to appoint (and pay) its own consultant. Any such appointment has to be made in consultation with the developer and the arts consultant must be acceptable to the other members of the design team.

ACCEPTING A 'SHELL' SPACE

Particular care needs to be taken when the offer of a 'shell' space is made as this is an area which has caused problems in the past.

The size, shape, internal volume, construction materials, and finishes all affect the way a space can be used for the arts, as do the means of access, the internal circulation routes, the position of doors and windows and the ancillary accommodation.

In construction terms the services also form part of the shell in that they need to be built into the structure as part of the main contract.

This means that any space which is to be provided for the arts has to be planned for that purpose when the overall scheme is being designed and not left as a 'hole' to be sorted out by the arts organisation at a later date.

Agreements need to be clear as to what constitutes the 'shell' and costings worked out so that the arts organisation knows what is to be provided and where its own responsibilities lie. People can be surprised at the cost of the remaining work - a 'shell' can represent little more than half the cost of the completed facility.

It is also important to determine who carries out the work and who supplies the equipment. The whole job can be undertaken by a single contractor (with the costs divided appropriately) or the arts organisation can be left to negotiate its own 'fitting out' contract once the 'shell' has been handed over.

ARTS ORGANISATIONS AS DEVELOPERS

As well as seeking to encourage public authorities and private developers to consider making provision for the arts in new developments, it is possible for arts organisations to take the initiative and promote commercial developments to help meet the cost of housing the arts.

The prerequisite for such a course of action is to have (or be able to acquire) space in terms of land or buildings which can be regarded as surplus to requirements. The criteria are the same as for any commercial development:

- there has to be a demand for the spaces which are to be sold or leased;

- an agreement has to be reached with the local planning authority;

- the commercial part of the development needs to be profitable.

The simplest form of commercial undertaking is the letting of space within an existing building for commercial purposes. This could be in the form of a concession to provide services required by the arts organisation (e.g. catering, sales) or it could involve letting out spaces for purely commercial purposes (shops aimed at the same user group). Depending on the terms of the original planning permission, even a development on this scale might involve a 'change of use' application.

At the other end of the scale, are the initiatives currently being undertaken by the Royal Opera House and South Bank Boards to develop adjacent land to help finance the cost of their own development programmes. In each case, there are a number of key factors working in favour of the projects:

- the sites are very attractive in development terms;

- the arts organisations are prestigious and are seen as assets to the boroughs in which they are situated;

- the board members have a great deal of experience and influence.

Even so, the proposed developments are not having an easy passage and serve to illustrate some of the problems which are likely to be encountered in achieving a density of commercial development which is sufficient to finance the arts buildings as well as being acceptable to the local authority and surrounding community.

WORKING WITH CONSULTANTS

This chapter looks at the use of consultants. There are two main parts:

APPOINTING AND USING A CONSULTANT
which discusses when a consultant should be used, how to select the right person for the job, the basis on which he/she is appointed and how the fees are worked out.

THE AREAS OF EXPERTISE
which lists the different types of consultants, the bodies which represent them and outlines their respective areas of expertise.

APPOINTING AND USING A CONSULTANT
The planning, design and construction of any building project draws on a range of skills and expertise. Guidance may be obtained free of charge at the early stages from local organisations and sympathetic individuals. Some of the skills required may be available within a group or company and existing staff can be trained in various aspects of the process. Very few projects, however, can be completed without commissioning a number of specialist advisors.

WHEN TO USE A CONSULTANT
Consultants provide expertise in a wide range of specialist areas. They may be employed to:

- undertake research and feasibility studies;

- develop proposals;

- carry out specialist procedures;

- advise on matters within their areas of expertise;

- recommend a course of action.

It is not their role to initiate overall policies or take decisions nor can they guarantee a successful outcome.

The technical skills which can be brought in through appointing consultants are vital to the success of the project. No existing building, whatever its apparent state and previous use, should be acquired without having the benefit of a full structural survey. No building work, except for very minor alterations and adaptations, should be undertaken without the advice of an architect. No new performance space or auditorium should be planned without talking to a theatre consultant or someone with a great deal of experience on the technical and production side of theatre work. No new visual arts facility should be provided without taking advice from someone experienced in the field. Money saved on professional fees can easily turn into a great deal more money wasted at a later date in rectifying problems which could have been avoided.

Where a legal matter has to be sorted out, it is advisable to appoint a solicitor. With financial transactions, an accountant's advice should be sought. Setting up a company, seeking charitable status, acquiring property and financing a construction project are all complicated areas of activity. While there are a number of useful publications which give an overview of what is involved, the details of legislation (particularly relating to tax issues) and the way the legislation is interpreted are constatly changing. This means that only those specialising in the field can keep fully up to date with current practice.

Professional fundraisers and public relations advisors also have a role to play but in these cases it is worth considering what the consultant can contribute which existing members of staff cannot. Fundraising consultants will not normally run an appeal but will help an organisation develop a funding strategy and outline a proposed course of action. Their advice is valuable in establishing a realistic target figure, setting a time-scale, identifying likely sources of funding and the amount or nature of possible donations, and planning presentation documents and techniques of approach. The decision whether or not to appoint a professional fundraising consultant depends very much on the nature of the project. Where a large amount of money has to be raised from private sources, the money invested in the consultancy may well be repaid many times over. Where the project is a relatively small one, or the bulk of the money is to come from negotiations with public bodies, the expenditure may not be justified.

Public relations advisers need to be brought in where there is a specific, identifiable problem to be tackled. Generally, arts organisations' interests are best represented by those who identify most strongly with their aims and objectives - the artists and arts workers associated with a particular project. There are a variety of skills involved in the presentation of a project and care should be taken to learn about these before deciding to tackle the job without outside help.

SELECTING A CONSULTANT
A consultant needs to:

- be properly qualified;

- operate independently;

- have expertise relating to the particular area of work;

- understand and be in sympathy with the client's objectives;

- be available to do the work when required.

Where an appropriate professional organisation exists, it is advisable to appoint consultants who are members of that organisation. This ensures that they are properly qualified, that they are insured and that the advice they give is impartial. (No professional consultant is permitted to form links with a supplier or profit from recommending a particular product or service.) The client is also protected by a mandatory code of practice and is given a specified level of service.

The selected consultant needs to be skilled in his/her own area of expertise and be knowledgeable about the area in which the client operates. A consultant whose previous experience lies outside the particular area of interest will have to spend time learning about the new activity, making new contacts and researching new procedures. Some of this time, at least, will be charged back to the client. Some firms of consultants offer a 'package' of expertise. While this can be helpful in certain situations, checks need to be made to ensure that members of the firm have the necessary range of expertise to cover all the specialist areas involved.

With a large scale project or one of a very specialised nature, the list of consultants needs to be drawn up on a national basis. For smaller and less specialised projects it is better to appoint people who work within the same region. They will be better acquainted with the practices of the area, whether these concern planning requirements or attitudes to funding and sponsorship, and often be more in tune with the aspirations of the local community. They will also have to spend less time and money on travelling (for which the client reimburses them) and be able to keep in touch with the project on a more regular basis.

Consultants, in common with the rest of the population, approach what they do from a particular point of view. It is, therefore, important to choose somebody whose approach is in sympathy with that of the individuals or group with which he/she is working. This is particularly important in the selection of the architect as the approach to the design affects, if not determines, the way the finished building looks.

Most of the professional organisations mentioned below provide lists of members who have the appropriate experience. The Arts Councils and Regional Arts Associations are also able to offer advice. When selecting an architect, it is worth looking at other new buildings, both for the arts and for other purposes, and finding out who designed the most interesting ones. It is not always necessary to choose an architect who has designed similar types of buildings in the past - many of the more innovatory projects are designed by architects exploring a new field. It is important, however, that the architect is supported by an experienced specialist consultant.

From the initial list, a short-list needs to be drawn up. This is achieved by making an assessment of the consultants' skills and experience based on the information provided and talking to their previous clients to find out what sort of job they have done. Where architects or design specialists are being selected, the client should take the time to look at one or two completed projects and/or photographs of work, to ensure that the design approach is in sympathy with his or her own ideas.

Before too short a list is finalised, it is worth checking that the consultant is interested in taking on the work and has sufficient time and resources available to carry out the job. It should be made clear that a number of people are being considered at this stage.

The final selection is normally made on the basis of an interview during which the consultant outlines his/her approach to the work.

THE TERMS OF APPOINTMENT
Consultancy time is expensive and needs to be used carefully if the maximum advantage is to be gained. Before any appointment is made, it is important to work out exactly what the consultant is required to do.

The contract of appointment needs to set out:

- the purpose for which the consultant is being commissioned - for example to research options for further discussion or to assess information already available;

- exactly what is required and the level of detail involved;

- the procedures for additional briefing, discussions and reference back;

- the time-scale for the job;
- the fees involved and the basis on which they are calculated.

Consultants work in accordance with their clients' instructions. It is important that they are given clear terms of reference and that there is a common understanding of what is required. Where consultants are working with an organisation, one individual within that organisation needs to take overall responsibility for their briefing.

The fees and terms of appointment need to be discussed at the selection stage. Most professional bodies have recommended fee scales linked to the services required. While highly qualified consultants, with specialist expertise, will charge more than their less experienced colleagues, the fees for comparable services should not vary greatly.

It is important to agree what the fee is, how it is to be calculated, what it covers and when it is to be paid. Fees are often based on an hourly, daily or weekly rate for the work done. This is an open-ended situation so it is advisable to place a limit on the time to be spent on a job or to negotiate a fee based on the estimated time involved.

Expenses such as travel, accommodation, printing, postage, telephone, etc. may be charged separately.

Where a set fee is agreed, it is linked to the amount of work to be done. It is important that the client specifies what the job involves as any additional work incurs an extra charge. The work undertaken on a client's behalf which is completed in accordance with his/her instructions, has to be paid for regardless of whether or not the client is satisfied with the result.

DESIGN TEAM FEES
By far the largest proportion of the money spent on consultants fees relates to the design of the building. The fees for design work are calculated in three ways. They can be worked out either on one of the following bases or on any mixture of the three. The ways are:

- on the basis of the time spent on the work;

- as a percentage on the equipment specified and designed by the consultants;

- as a percentage of the construction costs.

TIME CHARGES
For small scale projects the usual practice is for fees to be charged on the basis of the number of hours spent on the job. Consultants brought in for a short period to advise on one particular aspect also charge an hourly or daily rate.

PERCENTAGE ON SPECIFIC AREAS
Some specialist consultants base all or part of their fees on a percentage charge based on the cost of the equipment they design and specify. The mechanical engineer's fee, for example, relates to the cost of the heating and ventilation sytem. Similarly, a theatre consultant bases part of the fee on the stage, lighting, sound equipment, etc. which is installed in the building.

PERCENTAGES OF THE BUILDING COST
For medium and large scale projects, including conversion and refurbishment work, the fees of the various members of the design team are normally calculated as a percentage of the construction costs. The percentage figures vary according to the amount of work involved for each member of the team.

The percentage figures also vary according to the size of the project, the complexity of the work, and whether it relates to new buildings, refurbishments or conversions. As the size of the project increases, the percentage figure on which the fee calculations are based decreases. Arts buildings are regarded as among the most complex of building types with concert halls, museums and art galleries being placed in category 4, and theatres, opera houses and recording studios being placed in category 5 (the highest degree of design complexity) of the RIBA's scale. Most of the building team charge higher percentage fees for work to existing buildings than for new buildings.

Once the percentage figure has been established, it is divided into a series of amounts related to the work stages and is payable at the completion of each stage.

The fees are calculated on a percentage of the actual building cost. This is not fully established until the building is completed. Where earlier design fees have been based on an estimated cost which is lower than the actual cost, increased fees are payable retrospectively.

HELP FOR SMALL ORGANISATIONS
Professional advice is available to small organisations who do not have sufficient funds to pay the normal fees through groups working on a voluntary basis. What they are able to offer varies and depends on the resources available to them at any given time. Not all areas of the country are covered.

Free advice on the types of technical help available and on how to select technical advisers is available through the technical aid agencies. These comprise groups of architects, planners and surveyors who give their time free to help with community related projects. The Association of Community Technical Aid Centres will supply a list of centres throughout the country.

Business in the Community is a network of local businesses which are prepared to offer advice, services and, occasionally, personnel to voluntary organisations.

The addresses of the organisations mentioned in this section are listed in the Directory at the back of the book.

THE AREAS OF EXPERTISE
The main areas where advice is likely to be needed are covered by the following specialists. (The name of the main representative body is given at the beginning of each section. In most cases, these bodies provide information on fees and terms of the appointment and lists of members on request.)

ACCOUNTANT
(Institute of Chartered Accountants)

Most existing organisations retain the service of an accountant or have access to accountancy advice for the preparation of their annual accounts. Where a building project is being considered, financial institutions and many funding bodies require detailed financial information on the way the organisation operates and on the proposed work when applications for loans and grants are made. Accountants are able to advise on cash flow projections, loan facilities and tax legislation.

ARCHITECT
(Royal Institute of British Architects)

Architects are professionally qualified people concerned with the design of buildings. The title 'architect' is protected by law and may be used only by a person registered with the Architects Registration Council of the United Kingdom. Most consultant architects are also members of the Royal Institute of British Architects but this is not obligatory. The term 'architectural' is not legally protected so people offering 'architectural services' and 'architectural designs', etc. are rarely qualified as architects.

The architect's role is to work with the client to establish what is needed in terms of spaces and facilities and to design a building which will fulfil these requirements. The architect prepares the specification on which the building contractor bases his/her tender for the job and the detailed drawings to which the builder works. It is the architect's job to administer the terms of the building contract during operations on site and to inspect generally the progress and quality of work.

An architect may be employed as a consultant to assess the suitability of a site or building, to prepare an outline design or to carry out a feasibility study.

ARTS CONSULTANT
No organisation or representative body exists, although the Arts Council has a database of consultants, which can be consulted on application to the Marketing department. Arts consultants are an amorphous and changing group of people who have acquired their expertise through working in the arts - as creative artists, running companies and venues, working for national and regional arts organisations, etc. A few groups exist but, in the main, arts consultants work as individuals and their areas of knowledge tend to be specific rather than general. Collectively, their expertise covers a very wide area - programme planning, management and staffing structures, space and facility requirements, technical provisions, sources of funding, etc. across the building types and the arts forms. Advice will have to be sought to find out who is available and to identify the appropriate person for the job.

There is no fee scale. Arts consultants hold or have held senior positions in arts administration

and their fees will be related to a commensurate level of salary.

(See also 'Theatre Consultant'.)

CONSULTING ENGINEER
(Association of Consulting Engineers
Institution of Electrical Engineers
Institution of Mechanical Engineers
Institution of Structural Engineers
Institute of Acoustics)

Consulting engineers form part of the design team for major building projects.

- Structural engineers advise on the structural capacities of existing buildings and design and advise on new structures.

- Service engineers (mechanical and electrical engineers) design and advise on the installation of heating, ventilation, electrical work, lighting, lifts and related services.

- Acoustic engineers advise on sound insulation, the design and installation of sound control systems, and how the shape, materials and surfaces of a building affect the quality and movement of sound.

If they are to form part of the team working on a project, it is normal practice to make these appointments in consultation with the architect. Where an engineer is being sought to advise on a particular aspect (e.g. to improve the ventilation in an existing auditorium), the appropriate professional institute will supply a list of suitable people.

EXHIBITION CONSULTANT
There is no organisation co-ordinating people specialising in the design and equipping of exhibition and gallery spaces. A number of arts consultants, architects and exhibition designers have the necessary expertise to advise on new visual arts spaces.

FUNDRAISING CONSULTANT
(Institute of Charity Fundraising Managers)

With the change of emphasis from public funding to private giving, the role of the fundraiser has become increasingly important. The professional fundraiser's expertise lies in being well-informed on current practice, keeping in touch with legislation on sponsorship and charitable giving and advising on a range of sources of finance as well as planning and overseeing a fundraising campaign.

PLANNER
(Royal Town Planning Institute)

A planning consultant advises on planning law. In most cases, arts organisations seeking change of use or planning permission for a building would be adequately advised through discussions with the local authority planning department. Where a major new development threatened the future of an existing arts facility, a planning consultant might be brought in to represent the arts organisation's interests. There are also individuals and firms which specialise in 'planning gain' issues.

PUBLIC RELATIONS CONSULTANT
(Public Relations Consultants Association)

Public relations consultants will undertake research on what support exists for a particular project, suggest how this can best be mobilised and develop contacts with the press and media.

They can help with planning a publicity campaign, the design of information material and the style of its presentation.

SOLICITOR
(Law Society)

A solicitor advises on all matters which have legal connotations such as entering on any form of contract, setting up a company or registering as a charity. Solicitors also undertake conveyancing of property. (Changing legislation will enable other people and organisations, such as estate agents and building societies, to offer this service in the future.)

SURVEYOR
(Royal Institution of Chartered Surveyors)

Building surveyors are qualified professionals who are able to undertake structural surveys to advise on the condition of an existing building (fabric, foundations, services, etc).

Quantity surveyors work out the detailed cost of a building based on the materials and time involved in the construction. They form part of the design team and would normally be appointed in consultation with the architect.

THEATRE CONSULTANT
(Society of Theatre Consultants)

Theatre consultants are unique in that they bridge the gap between the arts users and the building design team. Their position is not defined by any formal training or qualifications, but regular practitioners belong to a professional organisation, the Society of Theatre Consultants which was set up in 1964 to maintain and promote standards. Its members all have a proven record in various aspects of briefing, planning and equipping a wide range of performance-related buildings, both new, by conversion or renovation. These extend to concert halls, conference centres, cinemas, recording studios, TV studios, and multi-purpose spaces, as well as theatres.

The specialist advice available from members of the Society includes management and feasibility studies, design briefs, general planning, auditorium studies and production requirements. Detailed technical advice covers the full equipment range from stage lighting and sound to communications, stage machinery and flying systems.

As well as offering technical expertise, theatre consultants can help to analyse the artistic and functional needs of users and define them in terms which can be understood by all members of the design team.

The design team for a performance related arts project normally includes a theatre consultant.

VALUER
(Incorporated Society of Valuers and Auctioneers)

Valuers may need to be consulted to give advice on the market value of a site or property. They are often qualified surveyors and part of a firm of estate agents, valuers and surveyors.

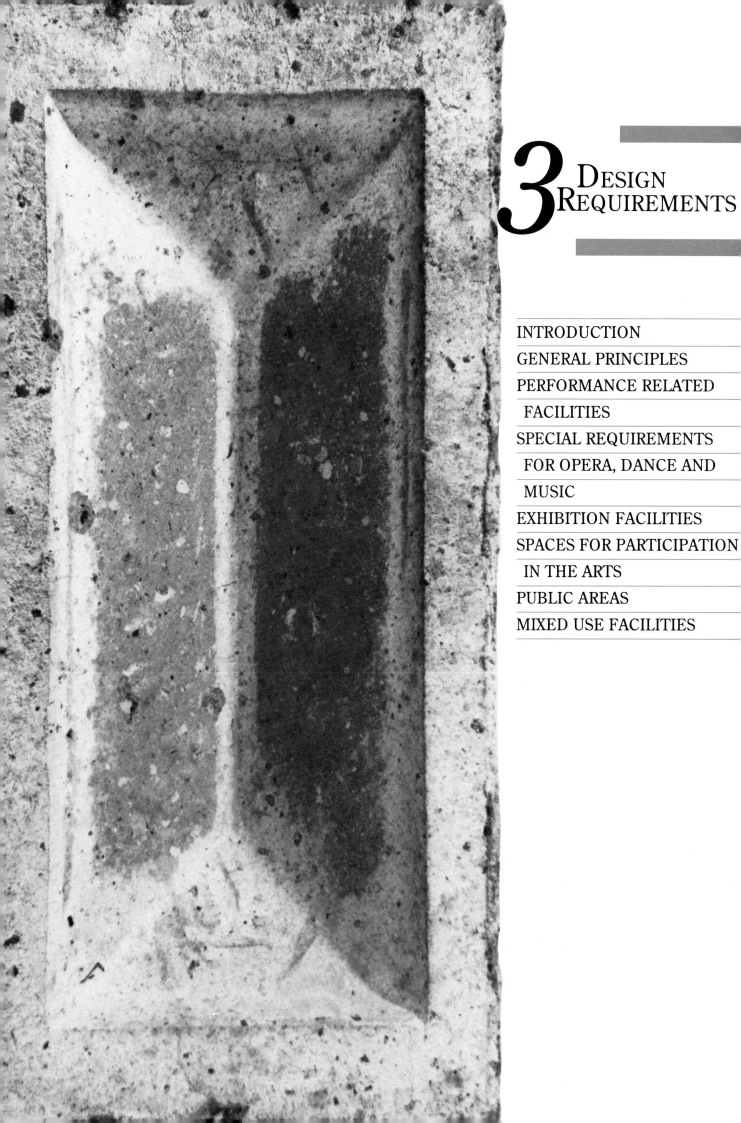

3 DESIGN REQUIREMENTS

This section sets out the basic requirements for buildings and areas within buildings, designed to house the main art forms. Its purpose is to give an overview of the range and type of spaces needed. It is not written as a design guide or to provide a checklist for a design brief. Where detailed information is given, it is intended either to draw attention to a particular need or to give information on areas where a specialist designer may not be involved - for example, fitting out changing rooms as dressing rooms, the use of staging units or the provision of a sprung floor. The first chapter, 'General Principles', sets out criteria which apply to the design of all types of arts buildings. Subsequent chapters outline the needs of the main art forms. The information is divided into three headings:

- 'Performance Related Facilities' which looks at the provision required in theatres and other auditoria based buildings (including halls adapted for arts use). Information on the special needs of opera, dance and music is included as well as notes on related non-arts uses;

- 'Exhibition Spaces' describes the needs of spaces designed for the public display of works of art and the support areas required in the galleries and arts centres which house them;

- 'Participatory Facilities' lists the types of spaces used for the practice of the arts (studios, rehearsal rooms, etc.) and outlines their requirements.

In addition to the areas for the arts activities, most arts buildings provide a range of public facilities including the entrance and foyer spaces, cafés and bars and shops. Information on these areas is contained in the chapter headed 'Public Areas'.

The section concludes with the chapter 'Mixed use Facilities' which gives guidance on the design of multi-purpose, dual use and shared spaces as well as suggestions for improving the arts facilities in public halls.

DETAILED TECHNICAL INFORMATION
There are a number of books which provide specialist technical information for those involved in the design of arts buildings and/or the preparation of the detailed brief. (See 'Bibliography'.) 'Theatres - Planning Guidance for Design and Adaptation' gives detailed technical information on all aspects of theatre and auditoria design. (It has been used as a source of reference for this section.) Written by Roderick Ham and published by Butterworth Architecture, it is now in its second edition (1987).

'The Architecture of Sound' by Peter Lord and Duncan Templeton, published by Butterworth Architecture in 1986, gives technical information on the design of concert halls and other music spaces.

No comparable book exists for galleries and exhibition spaces. The most up-to-date technical information is contained in articles in the specialist press. (The RIBA Library has a comprehensive indexing system.)

ADVISORY AND CONSULTANCY SERVICES
Theatre consultants offer specialist advice on all aspects of auditorium design and equipment. They may be brought in as consultants at any stage of the project from the initial planning to the detailed design. (See Section 2, 'Working with Consultants'.)

The Association of British Theatre Technicians (ABTT) provides an advisory service through its theatre planning committee. The committee may be consulted on any project which includes a performance space. Committee members have specialist expertise in all aspects of theatre and auditoria design. The most appropriate stage for consultation is at the beginning of the detailed design process. A fee is charged to cover the administrative expenses and a consultation needs to be booked about one month in advance.

NOTE ON TERMS USED
In the following text, the word 'workshop' is used in two ways. It normally refers to an activity in which groups of artists or artists with schoolchildren, students or other interest groups, work together to explore and develop some aspect of the arts. In particular cases, it is used to describe an area within a building in which equipment is put together (e.g. carpentry workshop, paint workshop), usually in the backstage areas of a theatre or in the support areas of a gallery. The context should enable the reader to identify the use of the term.

GENERAL PRINCIPLES

There are a number of criteria which apply to all arts buildings. These relate to:
- Designing for art
- Designing for people
- Designing for use
- Designing for economy

DESIGNING FOR ART
The most important element in an arts building is the provision it makes for the arts. To provide good facilities, those involved in the initial planning, the preparation of the brief and the design of the building, need to have an understanding of and enthusiasm for the arts.

PERCENT FOR ART
The visual arts and crafts have a place in all buildings, but have particular significance in those designed to house the arts. Through the promotion of the Percent for Art scheme, the Arts Council and Crafts Council are encouraging those concerned with the provision of buildings which are used by the public, to set aside a percentage of their budget for commissioning artists and buying works of art. The aim is to take contemporary art out of the galleries and formal exhibition spaces and make it an integral part of the buildings which everybody uses, day by day.

ARCHITECTURAL QUALITY

Architecture is one of the arts. In making provision for the arts the aim should be not only to provide the right sized spaces, adequately set out and equipped, but also to create a building which complements the activities which it houses and has quality in its own right.

When existing buildings are being improved or converted, it is important to respect the quality of the original. This does not mean designing a pastiche. There are many examples of refurbished buildings and additions to existing buildings which use contemporary structures and materials, successfully linking the new with the old.

FLEXIBILITY OR SPECIALISATION

Buildings are required in which the various art forms can each be experienced in the best conditions possible. Presenting a work of art to the highest standard can be a highly specialised activity which needs a purpose designed building, preferably dedicated to the single use.

At the same time, there is a need for arts buildings which can accommodate a mix of events and activities. The more specialised buildings also need to be used as extensively as possible to be economically viable. To achieve this, the uses to which the building is to be put need to be established at the outset, so that the necessary flexibility can be designed into the scheme. Some additional expenditure may need to be incurred to enable the building to adapt to a range of uses. (See page 85.)

DESIGNING FOR PEOPLE
THE ENJOYMENT FACTOR

In aiming to fulfil all the technical, legislative and economic requirements for a building, designers should not lose sight of the fact that the arts are there for people to enjoy. Arts buildings need to make a statement to the outside world, using the overall design, and the street facade where

appropriate, to celebrate the activities which they house.

They should be designed to welcome people, giving an indication of the feeling of 'an event' (c.f. the sense of anticipation generated by the circus tent). Once inside, the atmosphere should be a relaxed one. People go to a theatre, arts centre or gallery to enjoy a day or evening out. They want to explore what is available at their own pace, stop and talk to friends and linger over something which interests them.

THE NEED FOR COMFORT

Buildings designed for leisure activities need to be comfortable. The quality and layout of the seating, the design of the supporting facilities, the bar and refreshment areas, the ease of access and circulation all contribute to the comfort of the building in use.

Heating and ventilation are important. Air conditioning systems tend to be given a low priority in this country and can be one of the first things to go when costs have to be cut, as their cost accounts for a significant sum in the building budget and the end product cannot be seen. But a large number of people in a confined space will generate a significant amount of heat and installing a system once the building is operating will be considerably more expensive.

Those who work in the buildings also appreciate comfort whether they are performers, artists, technical or administrative staff.

ACCESSIBILITY FOR EVERYONE

Arts buildings need to be accessible to the whole of the community both in terms of the provision they make for the people with disabilities and in terms of the image they present to the inexperienced user.

The Arts Council's 'Code of Practice on Arts and Disability' sets out the standards it wishes to see

New entrance, foyer and restaurant accommodation in the extended Phoenix Arts Centre, Leicester (photograph by Burrell Foley)

implemented in all arts buildings. They apply to the whole of the building, including stage, backstage, workshop and office spaces. It is only when access to these areas is ensured that those with disabilities can participate fully in the arts.

Arts buildings should not be seen as 'exclusive'. Providing a facility which everybody feels is open to them, is largely a matter of policy and management style but the design of the building can make a contribution.

(Appendix 3 sets out guidelines on designing for people with disabilities.)

MAKING PROVISION FOR YOUNG PEOPLE

Education, in its broadest sense, is becoming an increasingly important part of the activities of any arts facility.

Circus Skills Workshop organised by the Magic Carpet Theatre at the Queen's Hall Arts Centre, Hexham (photograph by Caroline Reay)

For the last decade the Arts Council has been committed to developing the role of the arts in education. Initially, projects were promoted centrally but now all arts companies and organisations are encouraged to undertake this work. It is a two-way process. It involves artists taking their work out into schools and colleges, presenting their art to the children and young people and drawing them into activities which relate to that work. It also involves bringing the children and young people into arts buildings not only to see performances and exhibitions, but also to work with artists to develop their own ideas and skills.

When arts buildings are being designed, it is important to bear in mind that they will have an educational role. Some special facilities will be needed but most of the educational activities can be accommodated within the spaces provided for other purposes, with a few additions.

(See page 81 Educational activities.)

DESIGNING FOR USE
THE CONCENTRATED NATURE OF ARTS USE

Arts buildings have to cater for large numbers of people (whether at an exhibition or a performance) in a concentrated period of time. Where there is a performance, most of the audience (possibly 2,000 people) will want to enter and leave the building within a period of about ten minutes. During one or two short intervals a large proportion will want to use the toilets and get a drink. This means that the circulation routes have

to be very carefully planned. Cross routes (i.e. where groups of people need to go in conflicting directions simultaneously) should be avoided. It is also important to be aware of potential bottle necks and to anticipate queues and make sure they do not inhibit circulation.

The need to provide for concentrated use has to be taken into account when a building or site is being selected. Good access is needed, as well as adequate parking provision.

THE SAFETY ASPECTS

Whenever large numbers of people congregate, particular attention has to be paid to safety. Legislation governs the number, position and size of access and escape doors, the layout of seating and the width of gangways and corridors. Good escape routes are also needed for all technical areas, such as workshops, where flammable material may be stored. These areas should be separated from the public areas. In traditional theatres this division was provided by the proscenium wall and safety curtain. Where less traditional auditorium layouts are being used, careful attention needs to be given to the safety aspect.

Conflicts of interest can arise between the safety aspects and the overall design requirements. Early discussions with the relevant safety officers can help to minimise such conflicts.

ANTICIPATING EXTENSIVE USE

Arts buildings get very heavy use, which means that the finishes and fittings have to be robust if they are to last. Experience shows that the general wear and tear element is repeatedly underestimated. New arts facilities are often used far more intensively that their planners expected. (For instance, both the Pompidou Centre in Paris and the Burrell Collection in Glasgow have had success related problems in terms of maintenance and support facilities.)

Circulation areas get particularly heavy use as do the support facilities (toilets, bar areas, etc.) It is preferable to risk overspecifying in terms of quality (floor coverings, fittings) than to have to replace after a few years or put up with worn and broken fittings.

THE NEED FOR SECURITY

Security is an important factor in all arts buildings - not just the ones which display valuable (in insurance terms) works of art. Most arts organisations have expensive technical equipment - sound and lighting, videos and film equipment, as well as bar stocks and takings.

While in the interests of economy, the number of staff needed to run the building has to be kept to the minimum, care has to be taken not to isolate members of staff, particularly when they are handling money (e.g. box office, bar).

The design of the building needs to facilitate the closing off of areas which are not in use and to enable the staff to oversee the public areas. Some form of electronic surveillance may need to be considered.

THE IMPORTANCE OF GOOD STORAGE PROVISION

Most arts activities involve the use of a great deal of equipment (stage and seating units, sets, costumes and properties, exhibition screens, lighting and sound systems), only a proportion of which is in use at any one time.

Visiting productions and exhibitions have to be stored when they arrive and also before being sent on to another venue. Where a building is designed to have flexibility of use, storage is needed to house all the units and systems which are not needed for the particular format. Where a range of activities is mounted, storage is needed for the equipment they generate.

Good storage facilities can improve the safety of a building by helping to keep circulation routes clear. It is easier to clean areas which are not cluttered with surplus equipment. The risk of fire is reduced by appropriate storage being provided.

DESIGNING FOR ECONOMY

It is in everybody's interest, when a building is being designed, to try to make it as economical to run as possible without reducing the quality of provision for the arts or the public.

The costs of running a building fall into three main categories - staff, services and maintenance. Careful design and specification can reduce revenue expenditure in all three areas. Some of the ways of achieving this require an increase in the initial capital expenditure - for instance, where better quality fittings or more sophisticated electronic control systems are installed. The additional costs need to be set against the potential long term savings (calculated over a minimum ten year period).

ECONOMIES OF STAFF TIME

Staffing costs can be kept to a minimum by giving careful consideration at the design stage to the time involved in day-to-day activities - for instance, moving equipment round the building, or changing seating and stage layouts. Money spent on good mechanised systems can reduce costs in the longer term. The way staff are used also needs to be considered in the brief as the design of the building may enable people to undertake supervisory roles while carrying out their main work.

ENERGY AND RESOURCE CONSERVATION

The cost of energy to light, heat and ventilate a building is a major expense and one which is likely to increase in the future. Consideration needs to be given to selecting the most cost effective systems. It is often the case that the low running costs are linked to high initial costs. Highly sophisticated control systems using computer technology are being developed so that no more energy is consumed than is necessary to achieve a given objective. These are available for use in small scale units as well as for large buildings. Different areas of the building require to be controlled separately so that sections which are not in use can be maintained at a lower temperature and temperature controls can be set at levels appropriate to their use.

Good insulation (particularly at roof level) and careful choice of building materials can also reduce energy costs.

In the main, energy control systems are more effective than systems for creating energy (e.g. solar gain panels) though techniques may be developed further in the future.

The cost of water is going to be more significant in the future. The amount used is a factor which should be taken into account when specifying equipment.

EASE OF MAINTENANCE

The maintenance of a building needs to be considered when the brief is being drawn up so that the architect is conscious of the need to provide for ease of maintenance when detailing the building and specifying finishes and fittings. Ease of cleaning, accessibility and the frequency and ease of replacement all need to be taken into account. Any routine maintenance work which requires scaffolding to be erected, for example, needs to be kept to a minimum.

LANDSCAPING

Where an arts facility is set in its own land, it may be worth considering taking advice on planting and landscaping to make an attractive setting which requires little maintenance.

PERFORMANCE RELATED FACILITIES

All performance based buildings, irrespective of their size or complexity, share a number of common elements. They comprise:
- a main hall or auditorium
- accommodation for performers
- production and technical areas
- circulation and storage areas

The scale of the backstage provision relates to the use to which the venue is to be put. A producing venue needs a range of workshop and production spaces while a large scale touring venue requires more storage areas. The most demanding form in terms of backstage provision is the repertoire theatre as this needs to both create and store productions. (Definitions of 'producing' and 'touring' venues are given in Section 2 in the chapter 'Arts and Venues'.)

In mixed use and occasional use venues, the hall and many of the backstage areas can be designed to serve a number of purposes - for example bandrooms can double as rehearsal areas, whilst sports hall changing rooms can be used by performers if properly equipped and positioned.

MAIN HALL OR AUDITORIUM

The most basic provision for any performance space is a stage area and some form of seating. The way these relate to each other affects the

way the audience relates to the performance.
Different art forms and styles of production
require different audience/performer relationships. Visual and acoustic considerations also
affect the size and layout of an auditorium. The
format selected affects the shape of the main
space and that of the building as a whole.

AUDITORIA FORMATS
Most auditoria layouts are based on one of the
following formats. (Block diagrams are illustrated
on page 70.)

END STAGE (below)
A rectangular space with one end cut off to
provide the stage area. The seats all face the
stage directly.

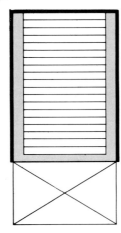

COURTYARD (below)
A rectangular shape similar to that of the end
stage but with additional seating ranged in rows
of galleries along the sides and back. The gallery
at the back is normally deeper than that at the
sides. The effect is to give a greater sense of
enclosure than is present in the end stage layout.
The members of the audience in the side balco-
nies are facing each other rather than the stage.

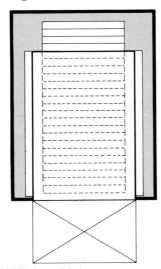

HORSESHOE (top right)
The layout is similar to that of the courtyard
theatre but the shape is rounded and the galleries
follow this to make a horseshoe pattern (the
stage forming the straight end). This gives the
same sense of enclosure with fewer people in the
audience seated at right-angles to the stage.

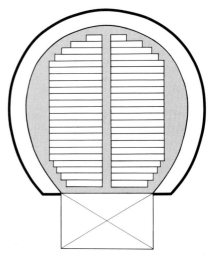

FAN (below)
The fan shape encompasses a range of layouts.
Up to an angle of about 90^0, the fan layout has
some of the characteristics of the end stage. As
the angle of the fan increases (up to 180^0), the
stage projects more into the audience and it takes
on some of the characteristics of theatre in the
round.

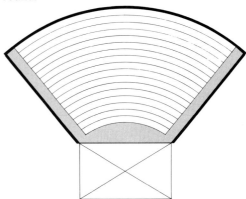

THEATRE IN THE ROUND (below)
In this form the seating totally encircles the
central stage. The audience looks through the
action across the stage to another section of the
audience. This arrangement suits a particular
style of production. A square format, with the
audience on all four sides of the centre stage area
can also be used to give a 'theatre in the round'
enclosure.

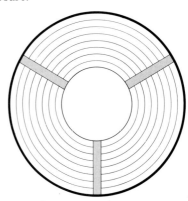

The seating can be provided on a single rake (a
sloped floor) or stacked up on one or more tiers

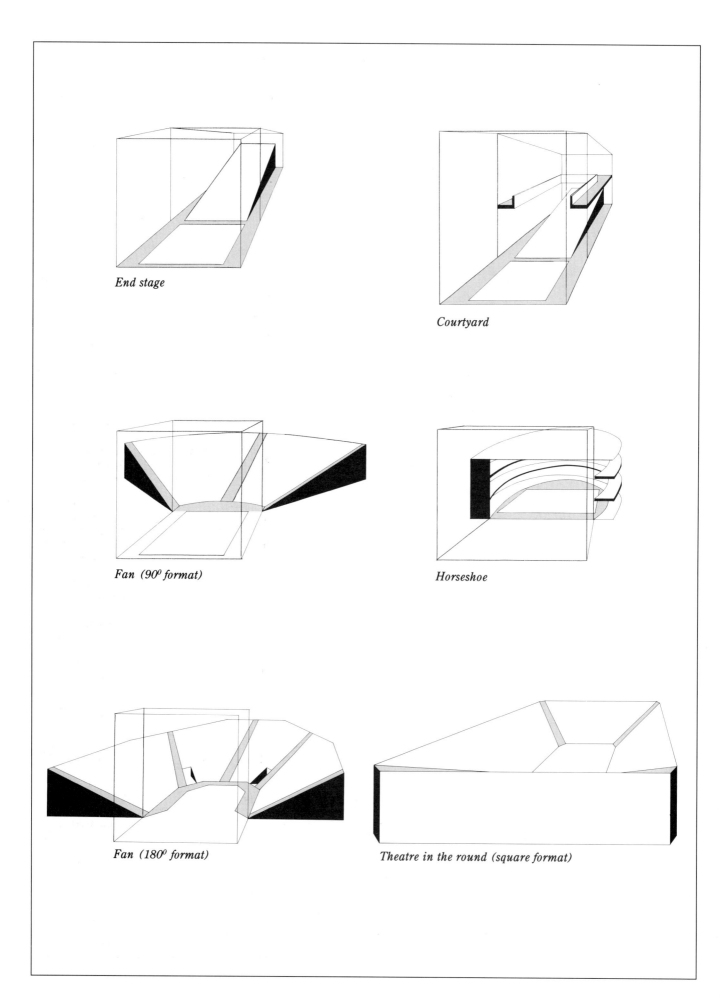

End stage

Courtyard

Fan (90⁰ format)

Horseshoe

Fan (180⁰ format)

Theatre in the round (square format)

above the main space. The tiers normally follow the shape of the main layout.

STAGE FORMATS

The shape and position of the stage relates to the shape of the hall or auditorium and to the layout of the seating. As the degree of encirclement increases, the stage reaches out into the audience. The theatre in the round situation represents total encirclement when the stage is completely separate from the back-stage wall and surrounded by the audience.

END STAGE

The stage is provided by dividing off a section of a rectangular hall. In a narrow space the actors may enter straight onto the stage. Where there is more width some form of masking can be introduced to provide wing space.

PROSCENIUM ARCH

The seating area is divided from the stage area by an arch (square or rounded) through which the audience views the production. This format provides wing space and enables flying systems (the means by which scenery is raised and stored above the stage area) to be used. This is the traditional stage format and many of the large and middle scale touring companies design their productions for this type of stage.

APRON STAGE

This is an additional section of stage in front of the main stage area in an end stage or proscenium style layout. It enables the action to be brought out towards the audience. Where an auditorium has an orchestra pit the apron stage can be used to cover the pit when it is not in use.

THRUST STAGE

This form of stage extends out into the audience. It is used where the seating layout is a wide fan or three-quarters of a square.

CENTRAL STAGE

This forms the performance area in the theatre in the round layout. It is often hardly differentiated from the surrounding area - possibly slightly raised. In a simple facility the floor of the hall could be used as the stage.

Both thrust and central stages place limitations on the amount of scenery which can be used. In neither case can the entrances of performers be masked or the stage cut off from the audience's view.

A number of factors influence the choice of seating and stage layouts:

- With an existing building, the dimensions of the available spaces dictate, to some extent, which formats can be used. Long narrow spaces may only be able to accommodate an end stage. Where there is a little more width, a courtyard solution could be considered. A large square space would suggest a wide fan shape with a thrust stage or theatre in the round;

- The layout of the hall or auditorium has an influence on the way it can be used - for instance, dance needs a large square stage area, films need a certain distance for projection, music needs space which gives good acoustics;

- Venues which depend on taking in touring product have to provide facilities which the available touring companies can use. In general, the small and middle scale companies are more flexible in their requirements than the large scale companies or the companies which tour productions scheduled for London's West End theatres;

- When an existing company is being re-housed, it will probably want an auditorium layout which echoes, or improves on, its established ways of working.

STAGE AREA

The stage need be no more than what the audience sees, a marked out floor space or slightly raised platform on which the performance takes place. The 'theatre in the round' and the simplest form of 'thrust' and 'end' stages may take this form.

It is more usual, even in very small venues, to have a stage area which provides access from the back-stage areas, waiting space, and cross over routes all out of sight of the audience, as well as wing space for the storage of properties.

In a major touring theatre, there is a substantial area surrounding the stage which provides space for large numbers to congregate (e.g. the chorus of an opera) as well as storing sets and properties for two or three productions simultaneously.

In many theatres, the stage area provides for some form of flying facilities. At its simplest, this is masked area above the stage which allows scenery to be lifted or rolled out of sight of the audience. More technically sophisticated provision can require a fly tower covering the whole stage area and rising to a height of at least double that of the stage as seen by the audience.

SEATING

Some of the factors which affect the choice of seating layouts and type of seating provided are sightlines, the relationship between the audience and the performance, safety, circulation, flexibility and comfort.

If the audience is to fully appreciate a performance, it needs to be able to see as well as hear. This means that some form of raked seating is required (i.e. where the seating levels gradually rise as they get further away from the stage). Raked seating is one of the most basic requirements for any performance space, however small and whatever the art form.

Gangways and transverse routes are needed to enable the audience to get in and out of the seats. The maximum number of seats which can be accommodated in an unbroken row and the minimum distance between the rows is governed by legislation and depends on the types of seating used. The width of gangways is also regulated in the interests of safety.

Where flexibility in use is required, there are various systems of bleacher seating available. 'Bleachers' or 'bleacher seating' is a system of stepped seating blocks which can be retracted for storage to provide an open flat floored space. Some halls are designed so that the whole of the seating can be removed. Others provide part fixed seating and part retractable or removable seating.

Bleachers need to be selected at an early stage as the type used has an effect on the design of the hall, including the positioning of access doors, circulation routes and storage facilities. Where these are already fixed, the choice of bleacher system is more limited. Factors to take into account when choosing a system are durability and ease of handling as well as audience comfort. (A theatre consultant is able to offer independent advice.)

LIGHTING AND PRODUCTION FACILITIES

All performance spaces need fixtures for lighting and sound equipment. Their position relates to the size and position of the stage. Where these are variable, the fixtures must offer equal flexibility.

The lighting requirements for drama, opera, dance and music vary, so if a space is to accommodate a range of productions it needs to be equipped with a full range of lighting facilities.

Some form of production control area is necessary. At its simplest, this can be an area within the hall or auditorium which is set aside to accommodate the lighting and sound control equipment with space for a single operator. More complex systems may require one or more control rooms, soundproofed and separately ventilated, which are able to accommodate a range of equipment and several operators. Whatever type of provision is made, those operating it need to have a good view of the stage, unobstructed by the audience, sets or stage masking.

Where films are to be shown, decisions about the projection requirements need to be made at the briefing stage as these will effect the design and positioning of the control rooms. (See page 76.)

House lighting needs to take account of safety as well as the ambience it creates. A secondary lighting system is required to give emergency cover.

ACCOMMODATION FOR PERFORMERS

Actors, opera singers and dancers require facilities for dressing and making up and for changing during a performance. Orchestral players and choral singers require more simple facilities for changing from street clothes into working clothes. In a small venue two communal dressing rooms, with washing and toilet facilities,

could be adequate. In a theatre or concert hall, a range of individual and communal dressing rooms and changing rooms is needed. The number depends upon the size and type of production to be accommodated. (See pages 74 and 75.)

DRESSING ROOMS

Dressing rooms need to be provided with make-up facilities with seating, work top areas, mirrors and good lighting. A full length mirror should also be provided in each room. Adequate storage for costumes (often fairly voluminous) and hats and wigs, is needed as well as secure storage for personal belongings.

CHANGING ROOMS

Communal facilities are acceptable provided they offer sufficient space and are properly fitted out. Separate facilities are required for men and women, but the rooms should be designed so that either sex can be accommodated depending on the nature of the production. They should be fitted with hangers and secure storage for personal belongings. Lavatories and washing facilities should be provided either as part of the changing rooms or easily accessible to them. A full length mirror should be provided in each room.

SHOWERS AND TOILETS

An adequate number of lavatories and washing facilities are required for performers. Showers are now regarded as standard provision. The number required relates to the type of activity. For instance, dancers and performers using body make-up need ready access to showers.

SPACE FOR RELAXATION

Known as 'The Green Room' (for actors) and 'The Bandroom' (for musicians), these rooms provide areas in which performers can rest and relax during rehearsals and between performances. (People can be in a theatre for most of the day and evening when a rehearsal is followed by a performance.) A smaller 'quiet area' is welcome in a large scale facility. Some access to fresh air and daylight is also appreciated.

Facilities for making tea and coffee should be provided.

Public telephones are useful in the backstage area.

PRODUCTION AND TECHNICAL AREAS

Some production and technical space is needed for every scale of performance space. Even the smallest touring company needs space to sort out equipment and costumes. A larger touring company needs areas to work on the sets and properties and a good wardrobe area. Producing companies need workshop spaces. These include:

CARPENTERS' WORKSHOPS, ASSEMBLY AREAS, PAINT SHOP AND RELATED STORAGE

These areas are concerned with the production of the sets. The requirements relate to the scale of the provision and the proposed working practices. Special attention needs to be given to all aspects of safety.

PROPERTY WORKSHOP AND RELATED STORAGE

A range of furniture and standard properties is often stored for use from one production to the next. Others are made specifically for each production.

WARDROBE

Space is needed to cut, sew and fit costumes and to maintain the costumes during a production. Laundry facilities are required as part of or adjacent to the wardrobe areas. Some office accommodation may be needed relating to the workshop spaces.

properties. Many use a range of large scale equipment. This has to be stored before and after the run and much of it needs to be accessible during the production. The height of doorways, lifts, etc. is as important as the other dimensions.

There is considerable time pressure on the delivery and repacking of the productions. Most companies move in or out of a venue in less than a day so spaces have to be clear and available.

STAFF FACILITIES

Performance venues have administrative, technical and production staff.

The administrative areas to be covered include: management, accounts, publicity and marketing,

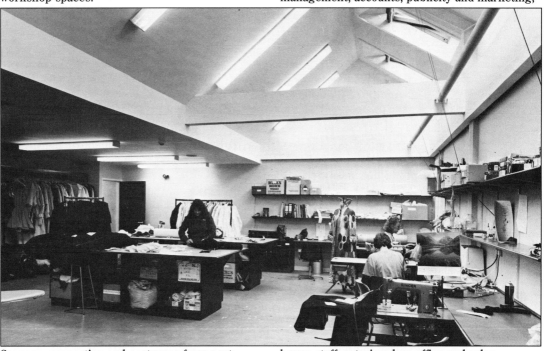

*Wardrobe work room
Perth Theatre
(photograph by
Cowper & Co)*

Scenery, properties and costumes from past productions are not necessarily stored in the main building. Where costumes are available for hire, the design and position of the storage facilities should take this into account.

ACCESS AND STORAGE AREAS

Performers and technical staff need to have direct access from the outside to the backstage areas. (Some form of security system needs to be installed if this access is not permanently staffed.) As well as the traditional 'stage door', access is needed for equipment lighting and sound systems, sets, properties and costumes. Where changes of level are involved, ramps or lifting gear needs to be provided. Narrow corridors with corners should be avoided.

Touring companies need parking and storage areas close to the backstage access. The vehicles they use range from the van (for a small scale touring company) to a series of pantechnicons (for a major production). These are often used as storage areas and should therefore be accessible during the run of a production.

Provision for storage is essential. Very few companies operate without any sets, costumes or

house staff, catering, box office and sales.

The technical areas include: the maintenance of the building and equipment, sound and lighting and projection, stage machinery.

The production areas cover the artistic directorship, design (set, costume, lighting, etc.), casting, reading scripts and everything to do with getting the production together.

The way these different functions relate to one another and to particular elements of the buildings is important. The position and grouping of the office space needs to take account of these working relationships.

Staff are often required to work long hours so good conditions and adequate support facilities should be provided.

OTHER FACILITIES

Theatres and other auditorium based buildings will often include studio spaces, activity based workshops (as distinct from the technical backstage work areas) and rehearsal spaces. Information on these is given later in this section.

SPECIAL REQUIREMENTS FOR OPERA, DANCE AND MUSIC

Opera and dance productions, can often be accommodated in the same spaces as dramatic productions, provided that some adaptations are made to suit their particular needs. Where a performance space is to be used for a range of art forms, this needs to be specified in the design brief.

Music normally requires separate purpose built (or specially converted) provision to be made if it is to be experienced in the best conditions. (There are some venues which are used successfully for both drama and music. These are either small scale or have been very carefully designed and technically equipped to adjust to the different acoustic requirements.)

OPERA

Opera is normally seen as part of the repertoire of a large or middle scale touring theatre, though some purpose built opera houses are now being planned.

SCALE OF PROVISION REQUIRED

The number of people involved in an operatic production is far greater than for any other performance at the same scale. A full opera company, for example, comprises a number of soloists, about 85 musicians (more for a Wagner opera) and some 60 singers in the chorus. Most opera companies include a small group of dancers. In the middle of the range, a touring company might have a chorus of about 25 singers and a orchestra of 55 players in addition to the soloists, and a small scale company could tour with a chorus and orchestra together totalling about 30 people.

A major touring company could take four productions on tour. At least one of these is likely to be a fairly lavish production. All this requires space for the singers and their costumes, space for the orchestral players and their instruments, space for sets, space for properties.

Conventional opera productions are expensive to mount and tour so they tend to go to large theatres with a good seating capacity (e.g. 2,000 seats) and even the small scale companies try to direct their work to venues seating 800 plus. Where opera is mounted in a venue with a lower capacity, the seat prices and/or subsidy levels have to be increased.

REHEARSAL FACILITIES

A number of rehearsals may need to be accommodated during the run in addition to the performances. Different sections of the company need to rehearse separately so spaces other than the main stage are required.

ORCHESTRA PIT

All large and medium scale opera productions require an orchestra pit, large enough to accommodate the appropriate number of orchestral players and their instruments (including a grand piano).

The acoustic requirements of orchestra pit design are complicated and specialist advice should be sought when making new provision or altering existing facilities. Normally, a proportion of the pit is built underneath the stage, with the rest extending out between the stage and the audience.

In most theatres, the only way an acceptable pit can be provided for operatic productions is to remove seats from the front of the auditorium. Unfortunately, it is the most expensive seats that have to be removed. It is the usual practice, therefore, to design the pit in two or three sections so that the full number of seats has only to be removed for the largest scale works. A mechanised lift system can be used to enable the floor to be raised and lowered in sections as required.

The separation which occurs between the audience and the performers is not desirable for most other productions. The pit is normally designed to be covered by seating or an apron stage when not in use.

In designing a pit, the aim should be not only to accommodate the appropriate number of musicians but also to provide them with acceptable working conditions.

DANCE

Dance companies share some of the special needs of the opera companies in terms of the numbers of people involved and the requirement for orchestral (or other music) provision.

SCALE OF PROVISION REQUIRED

A large touring company, able to perform the classical ballets, comprises 50-80 dancers and has an orchestra of between 45 and 60 players. (A visiting Russian company could be very much larger.)

MUSIC AND SOUND SYSTEMS

An orchestra pit is required for many productions. In others, recorded music is used. Good sound systems are needed as dance companies use both live and recorded music. Some companies may require the musicians to be accommodated on stage as part of the dance presentation.

SIGHTLINES

Good sightlines are important. Every member of the audience should be able to see the whole of the stage, including the dancers' feet, and as many as possible should be close enough to appreciate facial expressions.

STAGE AND FLOORING

Dance needs a large square stage (i.e. as deep as it is wide). 10m square is considered to be an acceptable size for most productions. The stage surface should continue at the same level, well out into the wing space to allow the dancers to run-off at speed or do a flying leap without landing in a trough full of stored equipment.

Most forms of dance require a sprung floor both for the stage and in rehearsal areas. (See note below.) Technical staff for one of the major dance companies recommend building the floor on a foundation of wooden bearers (two or three layers) in a 'basket weave' pattern. Strips of cushion flooring can be inserted at the cross points. The bearers are then covered with hardwood, tongue and groove flooring or ply-wood panels to provide the stage surface which can then be covered with a heavy canvas stage cloth or vinyl according to the needs of the particular production. A floor which is designed for dance can be used for a range of other activities though some uses (particularly where heavy equipment is being moved around) will damage the surface if the floor is not protected.

Note:
> Some South Asian dancers, and other groups of dancers who use the feet in clear, crisp, precise, rhythmic contact with the floor, do not necessarily require a sprung floor. In fact, some forms of dance work better without it.

BACK-STAGE FACILITIES
All performers need comfortable back-stage conditions, but for dancers these are particularly important. Above all, dancers need to be warm when warming-up, performing, rehearsing, changing and relaxing. If backstage conditions are too cold, this affects a dancer's muscles and can result in injury.

Adequate shower facilities are also important.

REHEARSAL SPACE
Dance companies need good rehearsal space within the building in which they are performing. The space should be comparable in size and shape with that of the stage (including wing space) and be of an adequate height for one dancer to lift another (minimum 14 ft. 4.27m). Daylight is desirable, a sprung floor, mirrors and fixed barre are essential.

MUSIC
While any auditorium based building shares a number of common elements, the specific requirements for music differ sufficiently from those for drama, opera and dance, to justify separate provision being made.

This section concentrates on the design of auditoria in which music is presented to an audience - concert halls, recital rooms and halls within buildings which can be used for formal concerts.

At the same time, there is a whole range of music for which the traditional concert layout is inappropriate. Music may be mixed with dance, with the audience participating in the presentation. In an increasing number of centres, particularly those directed towards a young audience, popular music is regarded as one of the main art form activities. Frequently there will be a bar within the auditorium and there are likely to be both live music and disco presentations with space for dancing as well as sitting. Such events can take place in the main hall or auditorium, provided it can adapt to an informal layout, or, if sufficient space is available, they can be accommodated in the foyer, bar or restaurant areas.

ACOUSTICS
Specialist acoustic advice is needed throughout the design process as the acoustics are determined by the overall shape and volume of the space, the materials used in the construction, the layout of the seating, the design of the stage and stage area and the finishes and fabrics used. When the building is completed it is likely to need some additional 'tuning' (i.e. making small adjustments to the acoustic provision to take account of how it sounds in use).

Increasingly, technologically based systems are being installed in music venues to adjust the reverberation times to differing sound requirements. They can also be used to improve the acoustics of existing halls. Some people, however, take the view that a truer sound quality can be achieved if the music is not processed in this way. It is possible to design a building in which physical adjustments can be made to the shape and volume of the interior spaces to change the acoustic environment to suit various musical works.

Where a building is being considered for conversion, it is worth mounting a range of music events (with an audience) to see how the building sounds in use, before any design decisions are made.

Channel 4 filming local bands at the Norwich Waterfront building before conversion work started (photograph by Richard Denyer)

SCALE OF PROVISION
Concerts and other music performances tend to fall into one of two categories:

LARGE SCALE:
1,500 to 3,000 seats. (See note below.)

A concert hall of this size is considered to be suitable for any of the large London symphony orchestras and the main regionally based orchestras, all of which tour the country.

The most demanding musical production, in terms of space, is a choral work with a large choir as well as a full orchestra. For such a production the stage and backstage facilities need to accommodate an orchestra of 100 and a choir of up to 200, as well as the solo singers.

A large concert hall of this size would traditionally have included an organ. There are now alternative, technologically based systems which may be regarded as acceptable.

MEDIUM SCALE:
600-1,000 seats. (See note below.)

A hall of this size can accommodate chamber music, song recitals, brass groups, solo performances etc.

Back-stage facilities are required to accommodate 40-50 people (including some soloists).

Note:
   The seating capacity is commonly used to describe the size of a venue. The suitability of a hall for a particular type of performance is related to a number of factors of which the seating capacity is not necessarily the most important (except in economic terms). The volume of the hall, the way the space is distributed and the acoustic qualities can be more important in determining the appropriate size of orchestra and range of musical works than is the number of seats.

STAGE AND SEATING REQUIREMENTS

While it is fairly common practice to mount musical events in flat-floored halls, most people enjoy a concert more when they can see the orchestra. When new facilities are provided, some form of raked seating should be considered.

or linoleum (this eliminates the possibility of the cellos getting stuck in between stage units) and should be selected (and properly maintained) to avoid creaking during use.

PIANO STORE

Storage space should be provided for a grand piano to give easy access to the stage. This should be in a secure place, preferably at the same level as the stage. Humidity and heat control systems are now being installed in piano stores.

NOTES ON FILM AND VIDEO USE

The design of a purpose built cinema falls outside the scope of this book. However, halls and auditoria designed for live performances are used to show films.

Not all theatre layouts are appropriate for watching films so if an auditorium is to be used for films, this requirement should be included in the architect's brief. Properly ventilated projection spaces, screening facilities and a good relationship between the projection room, the audience and the screen can then be provided.

Under the provisions of the Cinemas Act 1985, a license is required for any film exhibitions to be shown to a paying audience other than on a very occasional basis.

Particular attention needs to be given to health and safety requirements and to fire precautions in

Interior view of Nottingham Concert Hall (photograph by David Reed)

In a concert venue, the stage or platform is part of the auditorium, not cut off from it as in a proscenium theatre. The sound needs to be directed towards the audience so the traditional proscenium stage with its open fly tower space is quite inappropriate.

The stage itself should have a level and unbroken surface. Where staging units are being used in a small hall or multi-purpose space they should be covered with a continuous material such as vinyl

the projection area.

FILMING PERFORMANCES

When designing new arts buildings, it is worth considering providing facilities for productions to be filmed. As the number of television channels increases, so should the opportunities for live productions to be recorded for television.

The Arts Council is setting up an independent subsidiary company (Arts Council Television) to

Interior of the Countess of Huntingdon's Hall,Worcester (photograph by Peter Pritchard)

facilitate the broadcasting of the work of arts companies. It is planned to start operating in 1991/92.

NOTES ON CONFERENCE USE

The use of a performance space for conferences during the daytime or when no performance is scheduled is often seen as a way of bringing in additional income. To make a hall suitable for conference use two main points need to be considered:

- the relationship between the stage and the audience:

  the speakers need to be in close contact with their audience. There will also be question sessions when the speakers and the delegates need to interact directly. The traditional theatre form, where the audience is stacked in circles and galleries does not lend itself to interaction between the audience and the speakers. Layouts where the bulk of the audience is in a single area work better.

- acoustics and sound system:

  where a purpose built concert facility is being considered, additional sound systems will need to be provided to adjust the acoustics of the hall to speech. Systems are also needed to enable the delegates to communicate with the speakers.

Conference organisers also require film and video projection facilities. Some need facilities for translation.

NOTES ON POP CONCERT USE

The promotion of pop concerts is sometimes seen as a way of increasing earned income. The larger the auditorium, the more profitable they are.

Points to consider when designing for occasional pop concert use are:

- large numbers of people need to be got in and out of the building very quickly;

- seating and equipment in the public areas need to be robust;

- powerful sound, amplification and lighting systems are used. While the actual equipment is normally provided by the travelling group, fitment points are required in the stage areas and auditorium as well as an adequate power supply;

- the volume of sound produced will be greater than for normal arts use, which means that the building needs to be well insulated.

EXHIBITION FACILITIES

This section looks at facilities for the display of paintings, prints, sculpture, crafts and photography.

It concentrates on galleries and exhibiton spaces for temporary and changing exhibitions, where the emphasis is on the work of living artists. It does not cover the more specialist requirements of galleries housing permanent collections and museums of art where there is an important additional curatorial role. Advice on these aspects may be obtained from the Museums and Galleries Commission and the Area Museums Services.

DISPLAY AREAS

The display area or areas form the core of any exhibition facility. A large open space, or series of large open spaces is required, which can be subdivided as necessary.

THE SHELL

The walls which enclose the exhibition spaces need to provide large flat uninterrupted surfaces. They should be without windows. Opinion differs as to whether or not daylight is desirable in an exhibition gallery. Some people favour the completely enclosed box solution, artificially lit and ventilated. Others prefer some daylight, but this has to be indirect light, preferably at a high level. Bringing daylight into a gallery is easier where it is designed to house a permanent collection, as the nature of the material on display and the lighting requirements are fixed. A serviced box offers more flexibility for the display of works of art where the type and scale of the material is constantly changing. This solution does, however, restrict the range of alternative uses to which an exhibition space can be put.

One of the refurbished galleries at the Whitechapel Art Gallery, London (photograph by Martin Charles)

SERVICES

The provision of services is very important in exhibition spaces, both for the comfort of the public and for the care of the material on display. Once natural sources of light and ventilation are excluded or restricted, mechanical replacements have to be provided. Many works of art are only available for display where there are adequate controls on levels of lighting, heat and humidity. When this equipment is installed it should be selected and positioned so as not to interrupt the display areas. One solution is to provide a space between the ceiling of the gallery and the floor

above containing the servicing equipment. Where the floor to ceiling height is limited, ducting may need to be fitted to the walls or ceiling.

ACCESS

Good access is essential to get the exhibition material in and out of the building and to move it through the interior spaces.

If exhibition spaces are above ground floor level a service lift is required, large enough to take the display material. Where works are too large to be fitted into the lift, a picture slit can be provided (or trap for sculptures) with the necessary lifting gear, to move the works from one floor to the next. All doorways (including lift doors) and corridors used for access must be of an adequate height. Tight corners in corridors should be avoided as large flat shapes cannot be negotiated round them.

DIVISIONS AND SCREENING

In order to accommodate a range of scales of work, a system of screening is required. The screens used should relate, in style, substance and finish, to the surrounding walls. For large

Exhibition area in the Tate Gallery, Liverpool

scale works, large open spaces are required. Small scale works can be shown in a series of room sized spaces. Many exhibitions need a mixture of such spaces.

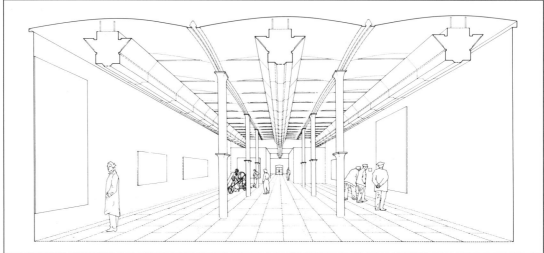

Drawing showing the ducting system installed to service the exhibition areas in the Tate Gallery, Liverpool (drawing by Stirling Wilford and Associates)

The system needs to be flexible. Both the exhibition spaces and the screening systems need to be designed so that the individual screens can be fixed in a variety of positions. The lighting fitments have to respond to the flexibility of the other elements.

The design of the gallery should enable a number of different layouts to be installed without inhibiting the flow of people through the spaces.

SURFACES AND FINISHES

Plain surfaces and finishes are normally recommended as styling details, patterns and textured finishes can conflict with the items on display. The exhibition areas will be hung and rehung many times a year. It is accepted practice to repaint the surfaces of walls and screens between each exhibition so a surface is needed which takes paint easily and does not retain the indentations formed by previous hanging and mounting equipment. Preferences as to colour differ. While some people prefer white, others think this provides too stark an environment and recommend a muted colour tone. Where colour is introduced, a light neutral shade is regarded as providing the best background for a series of changing exhibitions.

FLOORS

All floors need to be capable of taking heavy loads.

Floor surfaces need to be hardwearing (to take both the shifting display equipment and constant tread of people round the exhibition). They should be of a uniform character over the whole area to enable the layout to be changed around.

SECURITY

Security is important at all stages, both when works are being stored and when they are on display. Specialist advice should be sought either through the police or, where particularly valuable works are being handled, by contacting a security consultant.

WORKSHOP AND STORAGE SPACE

Workshops are needed for the maintenance of the exhibition areas and the production and maintenance of display material (screens, units, mounts etc.). Space is also required in which to pack the exhibitions. Access doors and ceiling heights in these workshops areas need to relate to the gallery spaces.

Storage is required for exhibitions which have just been delivered or are awaiting collection as well as for the packaging material while the works are on display. Space is also required to store exhibition equipment which is not being used (e.g. when a few very large works are being exhibited most of the screening, display units, lighting equipment, etc. is in store).

The packing and storage areas need to be easily accessible to outside parking facilities which should be large enough to accommodate a pantechnicon. If access to the workshops is not on the level, a ramp or lifting gear needs to be provided.

STAFF FACILITIES

Offices are required for the administrative, technical and custodial staff.

The administrative staff run the gallery, plan the exhibition programme, handle the publicity, catalogues etc. and control the finances. Whether this is done by a few individuals or a team of people depends on the scale of the operation. However many people are involved, some office space will need to be provided as well as space for storage and equipment.

Technical staff are needed to handle the exhibitions, organise the screens, mount the display material and light the exhibition. They need workshop and storage space and office space related to the workshop areas. Some office space adjacent to the working areas may be required. Lavatories and other staff facilities need to be accessible from these areas or separate provision has to be made.

Custodial staff are needed to watch over the exhibits. They require somewhere to store their personal belongings and somewhere to relax when off duty for short periods.

SPACES FOR PARTICIPATION IN THE ARTS

Much arts activity is participatory. It includes:

- the individual activity of creative artists painters, sculptors, dancers, musicians, actors, singers and writers;

- groups of artists working together to rehearse or develop new work;

- artists working with groups of children and students;

- groups coming together to undertake a joint activity (e.g. choirs, orchestras, bands, dance sessions).

Spaces for the practice of the arts can be provided within other arts buildings (in arts centres, theatres, galleries, etc.) or as separate units. The types of spaces used and the special facilities which are needed are listed below classified under the different art forms. A section is included on the provision of working spaces for educational uses.

In many cases the different art forms and activities can share spaces (e.g. rehearsal rooms and workshop areas) provided they are designed and equipped to meet each individual need.

DRAMA RELATED ACTIVITIES
WORKSHOP SPACES

Workshop spaces provide facilities for artists, working together or with local groups, to explore and develop a particular art form. Some rooms need to be large enough to accommodate large groups (possibly a class of children). Activities

*Rehearsal room/studio
in the refurbished Perth
Theatre
(photograph by Cowper
&Co)*

may include such things as mask and costume
making, set design etc. so worktop areas and a
heavy duty sink should be provided.

REHEARSAL ROOMS
These need to be large enough to reproduce the
stage layout with additional spaces for entrances
and exits to be made.

Teaching and practice rooms are used to develop
particular skills (e.g. voice or movement). Most
types of room can be used, provided they are
reasonably soundproof.

DANCE RELATED ACTIVITIES
Workshop and practice areas are used. Their
requirements are similar to those for dance
rehearsal spaces. (See page 75).

Any space which is used for dance has to have
adequate conditions in terms of flooring, height,
overall space and heating.

MUSIC RELATED ACTIVITIES
REHEARSAL SPACES
Spaces are needed where individuals and groups
can practice - small studios for single instrumen-
talists and rehearsal spaces for groups.

They should be reasonably soundproof, especially where there are a number of studios
together or where other activities are taking
place in the building. The soundproofing needs to
keep sound in to avoid disturbance to others and
to keep extraneous noise out to avoid disturbance
to the musicians.

MUSIC WORKSHOPS AND RECORDING
STUDIOS.
There is a growing interest in electronic music
though few facilities exist. Studio space is needed
with good sound insulation, sufficient space for
equipment and adequate power supplies. Security
also needs to be considered.

Recording studios require similar provision. They
can be a useful facility to include within a theatre,
concert hall, or arts centre.

THE VISUAL ARTS
STUDIO SPACES
Studios provide work spaces for painters, sculptors, printmakers and photographers. They can
be individual, communal, or shared. They can be
grouped together with shared support facilities or
can form part of a complex with a gallery space
and/or sales area.

The size, requirements and position of the
studios depends on the type and scale of the work
involved and the nature of the materials being
used. Communal or shared facilities can be useful
where the art work is the result of a process
requiring a range of equipment (e.g. print
making). Artists involved in large scale works
need ground floor studio space or a goods lift,
load bearing floors and adequate storage provision. Some artists need a three phase electricity
supply for their equipment.

Some natural lighting is desirable but most artists
are able to work with artificial lighting. For
photographic studios, a system is required by

Children's workshop in the Green Room at the Queen's Hall, Hexham (photograph by Caroline Reay)

which the light can be totally excluded from some areas. Normal practice is to insert a small lobby between the light area and the darkroom facility.

Services need to be provided to individual studios and a good drainage system installed for disposing of waste materials, including chemical waste. Some processes require special ventilation facilities to be installed.

EDUCATIONAL ACTIVITIES

Many arts venues now provide spaces and facilities for children, as small groups or in school classes, to visit and work with artists and performers. Some have specialist education units within their companies.

These activities require:

- space for meetings, rehearsals, and preparation;

- workshop facilities for making equipment, costumes, etc.;

- office and storage space (for equipment and work in progress).

It is an advantage if these spaces can have separate access and their own ancillary accommodation (storage, toilets, small utility area with sink and water supply).

In a small arts building, it is not always possible to provide separate facilities for education work and so those involved in this area share the available spaces with the other activities. In such cases, it is important to provide adequate storage.

SPECIAL PROVISION

Where groups of children are using a building regularly some special provision needs to be made:

- it is useful to have a room where they can

congregate to talk about what they are doing and also to eat packed lunches when the visit involves a longer trip;

- where they are using activity areas, work tops, mirrors, sinks etc. need to be at a suitable height;

- special attention needs to be given to safety aspects in any areas which children use;

- potentially dangerous areas need to be protected or made inaccessible to wandering children;

- most school age children can cope with full size lavatories and washroom fittings but it is useful to have a lavatory space which is large enough to accommodate a helper and is open to both sexes.

PUBLIC AREAS

The public areas form an important part of most arts buildings. They provide places for people to meet and spaces for informal exhibitions and arts events. They accommodate the support elements - information points, ticket sales, cloakroom facilties, etc. They can also be used to generate income.

This chapter looks at the activities which these areas house and design aspects which require special attention when building for the arts. The information is grouped under the following headings:

- Entrance and foyer areas

- Catering facilities

- Special facilities for sponsorship and support groups

- Shops and sales outlets.

ENTRANCE AND FOYER

The entrance to the building and the space between the entrance and the areas which house the arts activities is a key space in any arts building. It serves a variety of purposes:

PUBLIC FACE

This is the first part of the building which those who use it see. Whether or not it is intended to present an image to the public, it will do so, and this aspect needs to be carefully considered when designing or converting an arts building. Buildings which give no indication of what is happening inside, tend to put off the inexperienced user who does not know what commitment is being made by stepping through the front door. Information about the venue and a view through to a welcoming public space, can help to draw in the more wary members of the public.

ACCESS

The front entrance provides the main access route in and out of the building. Few arts venues use this entrance as the point of control for access into the arts events. It normally leads into an open space which provides a range of facilities for the public. Some consideration, however, needs to be given to overseeing the entrance point so that personnel are able to keep an eye on who is coming into the building and offer help if needed (information, help with access, etc.).

INFORMATION AND SALES

The foyer space usually accommodates the box office (advance booking and pre-performance) or ticket sales point for entry into an exhibition, as well as facilities for the sale of programmes, catalogues and publications relating to the arts activities.

Provision may also be required for a small sales area for confectionery with related storage. This could extend to the sale of coffee and/or light refreshments if the main catering facility does not form part of the foyer space.

Larger sales areas and franchise shops may be provided in this area. (See page 84.)

REFRESHMENT AREAS

Some sort of catering facility is often located in the foyer space. Where this is not the case, the facilities need to be accessible from the entrance area, without going through the arts activity spaces.

In some arts venues, a café/bar has been successfully incorporated into the foyer area, and is used for arts events. (See below.)

PUBLIC FACILITIES

Lavatory and washroom facilities are normally provided in the foyer area though these may represent only a proportion of the total number within the building.

Some form of cloakroom provision is also needed.

SPACES FOR ARTS EVENTS

The foyer area can be used as an informal exhibition space and for smaller scale drama and music activities. Where a sufficient amount of space is available, it can be designed to accommodate an informal performance space.

There is an increasing range of arts activities which work well in a cabaret style layout. Where a cafe/bar is included in the foyer area, it can serve as a venue for these events. More flexibility is provided if some part can be cleared to give a flat floored space for dancing (either as a performance or for the audience to participate).

CIRCULATION

Careful attention has to be given to circulation requirements, including means of escape, and to controlling access into the auditorium or exhibition spaces and into the non-public areas of the building.

Circulation can be helped by spreading the facilities out rather than concentrating them in one particular area. (In small venues, however, the number of staff available may mean that the box office, sales area and control points all need to be positioned in one unit.)

Clear signing helps circulation. It is generally more effective to design this as part of the overall concept rather than to add bits to the completed building.

CATERING FACILITIES

The bar and café/restaurant facilities form a key area in most arts buildings. They have an important role to play for a number of reasons:

- when they are properly organised, they increase the income earning capacity of a venue. There are examples of arts related catering ventures which contribute substantial amounts of income towards the overall running costs;

- they add to the attraction and enjoyment of an arts event as a day or evening out. One stop entertainment venues are increasingly appreciated by the public;

- a pleasant bar or refreshment area draws people in and encourages them to spend time in a building. This is important for small organisations which are dependent on voluntary help and can help to establish an arts venue as a core facility in the community;

- the bar and restaurant areas can provide a relaxed and informal setting for many arts events, where people enjoy being able to eat and drink during the performance. Events of this sort can help to bring in new audiences.

Some arts venues experience difficulties with their catering facilities. Some lose money through bad management, poorly targeted and marketed provision and dishonest staff. Others have found themselves taken over by groups who are not only uninterested in the arts facilities but are antipathetic to them. These problems are less

Lunchtime in the Lang bar and restaurant of Perth Theatre (photograph by Louis Flood)

likely to occur where the catering facilities are closely integrated with the arts activities and the bar and restaurant areas are seen as part of the one organisation. Nevertheless, there are examples of the successful franchising of catering facilities. Where this system is used, a careful specification needs to be drawn up to cover not only the economics, but also the style and quality of the provision.

Balcony and entrance to the Synchro bar at the New Victoria Theatre North Staffordshire (photograph by Red Gilchrist)

TYPES OF PROVISION
There are two basic sections of catering:

- the full catering service:

    This offers a meal for people attending a performance, visiting an exhibition or taking part in an arts activity. While some venues provide a table service it is more usual to offer a buffet style facility to cater for a range of requirements. Once a building is set up for this type of service, it can prove economic to open the catering facilities over longer periods. For instance, a theatre might provide lunches as well as early evening meals. In this case, the security and control of sections of the building which are not in use needs to be considered.

- bar catering:

    This can be a continuing facility or related to a specific event or performance. The serving of refreshments and drinks immediately before a performance and during the intervals is a more specialised activity, as large numbers of people need to be served quickly.

    The traditional solution is to provide a very long narrow bar. An alternative is to attempt to spread the audience by providing a number of small bars. Both these solutions require a number of competent bar staff to be available over a short period of time. The advantages of a centralised bar facility in terms of providing stores, a single link to the barrels, washing-up facilities, etc. need to be balanced against the advantages of being able to spread clients over several outlets to avoid congestion.

SOURCES OF ADVICE
When providing a major catering facility it is advisable to seek specialist advice on the equipment specification and layout of the kitchen, stores and related spaces. This advice is available from commercial catering and kitchen design consultants whose main area of work is within the hotel industry. When selecting a consultant, checks should be made as to whether he or she is independent or linked to a particular manufacturer or supplier.

BAR INSTALLATIONS
Many brewery firms have staff who are available to advise on the design and layout of bars. They may also offer loans or sometimes undertake the work of fitting out the bar area in return for an

Riverside restaurant at Watermans Arts Centre, Brentford (photograph by Chris Arthur, Transworld Eye)

agreement on the barrelage to be taken by the venue over a given period. Such agreements can prove beneficial to organisations with limited resources but they need to be negotiated carefully. For example, it could be more advantageous in the long term to negotiate a discount on future orders and use the money saved to pay off a straight commercial loan.

Areas to watch are:
- the limitations placed on what other brands can be sold;

- the control of prices to be charged;

- the barrelage which has to be purchased (whether this is fixed or increasing over a period);

- the design of the bar (a particular brewery's house style can conflict with that of the rest of the building).

CHECKPOINTS
Specific points to be aware of when designing catering facilities in arts buildings include:

- Noise levels

   Catering facilities need to be carefully sited so that the normal actvities of setting up the bar, clearing plates and glasses, washing up etc. do not interfere with the enjoyment of the arts events. If the bar staff are to be used

efficiently they will not be able to wait for the end of a performance before they start to clear.

This also applies where a catering facility is open to the general public or serves a number of different events within the same building. Care has to be taken at the design stage to ensure that the bar can operate normally without disturbing any other activity.

- Security

   If a catering operation is open to the general public, some systems need to be installed to prevent access to the rest of the building, particularly when no arts events are scheduled.

- Style

   The catering areas should be seen as part of a building for the arts. The design of these areas needs to relate to that of the rest of the building and the style of service and management should be in keeping with it.

   Individuality of approach and a relaxed atmosphere are two of the attributes which contribute to making an arts catering facility attractive to both arts patrons and more general users.

SPECIAL FACILITIES FOR SPONSORSHIP AND SUPPORT GROUPS

Business sponsorship has played an increasing role in financing the arts over the last decade and it is the current Government's policy (1990) that it should continue to do so.

Sponsorship tends, in the main, to be directed to the more prestigious events though there are several major organisations which make contributions to community based projects as a matter of policy.

The 'prestigious' type of events sponsorship is likely to be easier to obtain where an arts organisation is able to offer some benefits to attract the sponsoring organisation. This could mean including a private entertainments suite within an arts facility. Such provision should only be considered in a large centre promoting the sort of event likely to attract major companies. The facility should be designed so that it can also be used as support space for conferences and/or as a separate function area which can be hired out for receptions, parties etc.

Where less ambitious facilities are required to entertain groups of sponsors to provide an additional attraction for those who join a friends or support group, the bar could be designed so that one section can be separated off for special events.

SHOPS AND SALES OUTLETS

Arts buildings have traditionally included sales areas. In the theatres there were small kiosks selling programmes and snacks for the performance. Galleries sold postcards and sometimes a selection of prints. Many venues will continue to want sales areas to cater for this limited scale of operation.

In other centres, the concept of 'arts related shopping' is being developed to provide an additional source of income. Where the venue operates its own shop, quite a large area may be required to accommodate a range of goods linked to the main activities of the venue. For instance, an arts centre might sell a range of books, records, craft works and craft materials, paintings and prints, artists materials, dance wear, etc. In many areas of the country, there is a dearth of specialist shops offering the goods in this range, so well managed provision can supply a need and bring in an income.

If the shop is to make a profit, the whole operation has to be carried out with as few staff as possible. The shop area has, therefore, to be carefully designed so that all parts can be seen and controlled from the cash point. Secure storage is also required.

Where an arts facility has some surplus space, there may be potential for letting out one or more areas to provide for shops on a commercial basis. With new arts developments, the concept of 'balanced development' is being introduced which provides for commercial leisure related provision to be developed alongside arts provision so that the one can help support the other. (See page 55, 'Development Opportunities and Planning Gain'.)

In all cases, care needs to be taken to ensure that the overall design of the spaces and their furnishings and fittings, the design and quality of the goods on sale and type of service provided in the commercial areas matches that offered by the arts provision.

*The bookshop at the
Tate Gallery, Liverpool*

MIXED USE FACILITIES

The idea of being able to provide a single multi-purpose space which can be adapted to accommodate a wide range of arts productions as well as other income earning activities is an attractive one. It is, however, much easier to achieve in theory than in practice.

This chapter looks at the problems related to providing multi-purpose spaces, both large and small scale and outlines some possible solutions. These include limiting the range of uses and providing separate spaces with shared support facilities.

It concludes with a series of notes on the design of buildings which provide for a mix of arts and non-arts uses including sports/arts facilities, public halls and arts provision in rural areas.

MULTI-PURPOSE AND SHARED PROVISION

MULTI-PURPOSE AUDITORIA
If a single hall or auditorium is to cater for a wide range of arts uses it needs to be able to adapt in a number of ways. These include the ability to:

- alter the scale of the overall space;

- expand and reduce the seating capacity;

- change the size and position of the stage (and the related lighting, sound and production facilities);

- change the layout of the seating and the relationship between the seating and the stage areas;

- adapt the acoustic qualities.

If exhibitions and a range of other uses (conferences, discos, receptions, etc.) are to be catered for, further flexibility may be required to:

- provide a large flat-floored space;

- increase the range of lighting positions;

- bring catering into the hall or auditorium;

- alter the circulation routes;

- introduce daylight.

Making a building sufficiently adaptable to suit a wide range of uses requires considerable design ingenuity as well as a substantial capital and revenue budget. Capital is needed to instal the mechanised systems which enable changes in spaces and layouts to be made and revenue expenditure is incurred in maintaining and operating these systems once they are installed. Opinions differ as to whether the standards which can be achieved justify the expenditure involved.

Anyone considering pursuing this option is advised to visit a range of multi-purpose and adaptable venues to look at what provision has been made, see how it is used in practice and take advice on capital and operating costs. While there are a number of facilities designed to cater for more than one use, those which can be regarded as genuinely multi-purpose are very few. The two best known examples are the Derngate Centre, Northampton and the Theatre Royal, Plymouth, which take different approaches to the problems of providing for a range of uses. The Derngate Centre is a highly adaptable building with a sophisticated system of units moved about on pneumatic castors. The units can be positioned to achieve changes in both scale and staging and seating formats. The Theatre

The Derngate Centre, Northampton (photograph by Richard Turpin)

Royal, Plymouth is designed to house a regional theatre company, take in the major touring productions (including those which require the traditional flytower and proscenium arch format) and provide a concert facility. This is achieved by designing an adaptable building in which the scale of the main auditorium can be reduced by means of a moveable ceiling which can be lowered to cut off one tier of seating. A system of assisted resonance adjusts the acoustics for the different uses. Neither of these buildings attempts to accommodate the full range of uses in a single space. The Derngate Centre is sited alongside the existing Victorian theatre, housing the regional repertory company. The Theatre Royal, Plymouth includes a second auditorium for smaller scale and less formal productions.

LIMITED USE SOLUTIONS
More limited finance may require the range of options to be reduced to a few uses which are either naturally compatible or can be accommodated in a space which is designed to offer some flexibility.

It is difficult to give guidelines as to which activities can be safely put together. With arts events, compatibility depends on the scale and style of production as much as on the art form.

As a general principle, a mixed use building needs to be designed to sufficient standards to cater for the most exacting of the proposed uses, even when this use is a subsidiary one.

- a multi-purpose hall which is to be used for the occasional concert needs to provide suitable acoustics for that use;

- a theatre space can be modified to double as a cinema and/or a conference hall but not vice versa;

- a floor or stage area designed for dance can be used for a range of other activities (drama, music, some sports and community uses) but a standard all-purpose floor or stage may not be suitable for dance.

This means that the range of uses has to be established at the briefing stage so that the design can take the specific requirements of each into account.

SHARED SUPPORT FACILITIES
Some arts buildings provide a range of spaces, with shared support facilities, rather than a single multi-purpose space. In certain situations this could be a less expensive option. Two or more halls or auditoria can be designed with shared back-stage areas, administration areas, access and booking facilities and restaurant/bar/foyer space.

The West Yorkshire Playhouse, the National Theatre, the Nottingham Theatre Royal and Concert Hall and the Barbican Centre are examples of multi-auditoria venues.

SMALL HALL FACILITY
There are a number of examples of small scale spaces which function reasonably well for a range of uses. Two thirds of the arts centres in this country function round a single large space which has to be able to accommodate a wide range of activities. To a certain extent, the small touring companies have adapted their work to suit these

Christ's Hospital Arts Centre, Horsham, with the seating set out to give a large flat floored area (photograph by Bruno de Hamel for the 'Architectural Review')

spaces and limited their need for special provision. A well designed small hall can, therefore, take a good proportion of the product available at that scale.

A flat floored hall with partial or full bleacher seating can be arranged to serve a number of different uses - a range of drama and dance productions (provided a sprung floor can be incorporated), music performances, workshops, community based activities and some income earning events such as discos, fairs, cabaret style evenings, etc. While it is possible to incorporate stage and and seating systems which offer great adaptability in both layout and scale, in most situations it is preferable to go for more simple solutions. The most commonly used formats are the end-stage or narrow fan layout (with raked seating) and the large flat-floored open space. These two options can be provided in a single hall without too much complexity by using a system of retractable seating (bleachers).

Where sufficient space is available, it is worth considering providing the upper part of the seating on a fixed rake built into the hall. This enables a flat floored area to be provided without removing all the seats. The fixed rake can be designed to allow the area underneath to be used for other purposes for example, cloakrooms, storage or a bar.

The stage area can be provided in a number of ways:

- with removable stage units

- using the floor of the hall

- on a built-in platform

In providing a stage area, the advantages of the flexibility to be achieved by using removable stage units need to be set against the disadvantages. Removable stage units have to be carried round the building and stored when not in use. This takes up both staff time and valuable space. If units are used, they need to be of good quality so that they do not warp with wear, creak in uses or shift with movement. When in use they need to be covered in order to provide a firm, continuous surface.

In some seating layouts, the floor of the hall can be used for the stage, though it needs to be sprung if it is to be used for dance.

Where a fixed stage is provided, it offers more flexibility if it can be made large enough to provide a flat floored area for non-performance activities, such as workshops.

A small hall may be used for exhibitions (other than those requiring high levels of environmental and security controls). In this case lighting and screening need to be provided.

Natural lighting can be an advantage for flexibility in use - for example day-time community use such as playgroups or after-school activities, arts classes and workshops, meetings etc. On the other hand, if windows are provided, it may then be difficult to exclude the light during performances and to provide an adequate level of sound insulation.

Storage almost inevitably presents a problem. The wider the range of uses to which the spaces are put, the greater the need for storage. This is particularly important in arts centres where a flexible programme frequently requires a wide range of equipment to be available but not necessarily in use. There is also a frequent need to store work in progress from educational activities or community events. Seating and stage units need to be stored when the flat-floored layout is in use.

NOTES ON MIXING ARTS WITH OTHER USES
THE SPORTS/ARTS MIX

The Sports Council and the Arts Council both take the view that, with careful planning and efficient management, sports and arts activities can be successfully housed together in the same building and that this could be the best option where separate, specialised facilities cannot be justified. The booklet 'Getting it Together' produced by the Sports Councill in co-operation with the Arts Council gives guidance on the planning, design and management of joint facilities and outlines some of the benefits which can come from mounting sports and arts activities in the same building. It is available free from either organisation.

A number of basic facilities are required to mount an arts event including removable raked seating, stage units, lighting grids, blackout systems, access to the stage and some backstage provision. The section on performance related spaces (page 68) gives more information on what needs to be provided and the booklet 'Getting it Together' sets out the requirements in the context of a dual use building.

Other design aspects which need special consideration include:

- Circulation

  The access and movement of people for large scale arts events create very different problems from those of everyday sports use. Sports use tends to be low density over a long period whereas arts use tends to be high density over a short period.

- Storage

  As in all multi-purpose and flexible use buildings, adequate storage is essential. This is particularly so in sports/arts buildings where each use requires substantial amounts of specific and separate equipment.

- Bar and café

  An audience for an arts event will appreciate good refreshment facilities both before and during the production. These should be easily accessible but should not be so close to the main halls to interfere with the arts event (i.e. noise levels) especially if they are to continue to open to non-arts users during a performance.

- Lavatory provision

There should be adequate toilet facilities. Those situated in the back-stage areas will not be accessible to the public during a performance.

- Simultaneous or alternating use

If sports and arts activities are to be accommodated simultaneously special demands are placed on the design and layout of the building. For instance, separate access may be required for each activity area, and additional toilets and changing areas may well have to be provided. Sports facilities such as squash courts and swimming pools need to be carefully sited to protect the arts use from unacceptable noise levels. In a small to medium sized sports building, it may be preferable to design for only one use (sports or arts) to take place at any one time.

- Safety

Arts use often requires additional means of escape and other safety provision. The division of the building into main use and backstage may make some of the existing means of escape inaccessible to the public. The position of the stage needs to be considered when the building is being designed so that it does not block escape routes.

ADAPTING PUBLIC HALLS FOR ARTS USE

Many buildings have a hall or other space which can be used to accommodate arts events. Schools and colleges, libraries, churches and church halls, public buildings, foyers and rooms in commercial buildings and rooms in large houses (e.g. English Heritage or National Trust properties) can provide space for festivals and one-off productions or exhibitions.

Some of the problems relating to the use of such buildings are organisational. Where these can be solved sufficiently for a building to be used regularly as an arts venue, it is worth looking at how the facilities for the arts can be improved. Relatively small amounts of capital investment may help to achieve this.

Experience shows that the following areas are the ones most likely to cause problems. They relate, in the main, to the needs of the performing arts:

- Sight-lines
  To enjoy a production, people need to be able to see what is happening. The widely used flat floor and raised stage layout cannot achieve satisfactory sightlines. Some form of raked seating is required. (Retractable or portable systems enable the hall to be returned to a flat floored area.)

- Blackout facilities
  Most performances, including the showing of films, require external light and light from the rest of the building to be excluded.

- Back-stage areas
  While some small touring companies have adapted to giving performances in a single open space, more formal productions require a backstage area which has a route to the

'Last Night of the Proms' in the main sports hall of the Sands Leisure Centre, Carlisle

stage without going through the main body of the audience.

- Access
  Separate access is needed for back-stage and front-of-house;

  Touring Groups need to be able to park close to the hall as the van doubles as a store;

  Equipment needs to be got in and out of the building;

  Escape routes need to be accessible to performers and audience;

- Storage
  All arts related activities (performances, exhibitions, workshops, etc.) rely on equipment which needs to be stored;

  Some storage is required in back-stage areas for use during a production;

- Lighting
  A space which is to be regularly used for arts events needs to be fitted with some form of lighting grid system;

- Lavatories
  Adequate toilet facilities are required both for the public and back-stage areas;

- Bar/refreshment area
  some provision for the sale of refreshments is appreciated by the public and also helps to increase the income.

ARTS PROVISION IN RURAL COMMUNITIES

Earlier sections of this book discuss the need to identify catchment areas and potential audiences before considering the type of building to be provided. Rural areas present a special case. The more scattered nature of the population means that the natural centres may never be able to draw upon sufficient numbers of people to justify larger scale or more specialist provision. If the people in these areas are to have access to a range of arts activities, other solutions have to be sought.

Arts activities in rural areas tend to be smaller scale and/or spasmodic. This means that use has to be made of existing buildings and that any new provision which is made needs to be designed to accommodate other uses.

In discussing the arts in rural communities, people often think in terms of 'recommended minimal provision', seeking guidance on a standard box which will accommodate a range of arts uses. Designing an arts facility for a rural area does not differ substantially from designing any other arts facility. The problem is not one of designing down for small scale use but in providing good facilities for use on a part-time basis. The solution lies in establishing a compatible mix of non-arts activities to ensure that the building is used sufficiently to justify its costs. This mix will vary from one part of the country to another as it needs to respond to local interests and to fill in gaps in existing provision.

AVAILABILITY OF PRODUCT
There are a number of initiatives taking place to extend the range of 'arts product' which can be made available to areas with a low population density. Many of these are listed in the Arts Council's recent report 'Think Rural: Act Now.'* The Regional Arts Associations, which have rural populations within their areas, are seeking to develop more work and many of them are able to advise on the range of activity available.

SOURCES OF ADVICE AND INFORMATION
The organisation ACRE (Action with Communities in Rural England) is also working to improve facilities and services in rural areas. It has published a series of leaflets giving information on the design of village halls and is planning a new publication entitled 'Village Halls: Venues for the Arts' with the support of the Arts Council.

The Rural Development Commission has published 'Multi-purpose village centres a study of their feasibility, design and operation' (1981).

(Details of these and other relevant publications are given in the bibliography.)

*('Think Rural: Act Now: A report for the Arts Council on the arts in rural areas'. Sally Stote 1989)

ARTS
BUILDINGS 1

CHECKLIST OF ARTS BUILDINGS

PERFORMANCE BASED BUILDINGS:

DANCE AND DRAMA

Building	Region	New Building	Conversion	Improvement/Refurbishment	Large	Medium	Small	Special Features
New Towngate Theatre, Basildon	Eastern	■				■		Adaptable main space
Theatre Royal, Bath	South West			■		■		
Birmingham Hippodrome	West Midlands			■	■			Good dance facilities
Alhambra Theatre, Bradford	Yorkshire			■	■			
Dundee Repertory Theatre	Scotland	■				■		'Infill' site
Citizens Theatre, Glasgow	Scotland			■		■		
Spring Street Theatre, Hull	Lincolnshire & Humberside		■				■	Low cost
Wolsey Theatre, Ipswich	Eastern	■				■		
Tricycle Theatre, Kilburn, London	Greater London	■					■	
West Yorkshire Playhouse, Leeds	Yorkshire	■				■		Adaptable second audiorium
Palace Theatre, Manchester	North West			■	■			
Royal Exchange Theatre, Manchester	North West		■			■		Adaptable module solution
Theatre Royal, Newcastle	Northern			■	■			
Theatre Royal, Nottingham	East Midlands			■	■			Linked to concert hall
Perth Theatre	Scotland			■	■			
New Victoria Theatre, Stoke	West Midlands	■				■		Theatre in the round
Grand Theatre, Swansea	Wales			■	■			New back-stage areas

MUSIC

Building	Region	New Building	Conversion	Improvement/Refurbishment	Large	Medium	Small	Special Features
The Junction, Cambridge	Eastern	■				■		Live music for young audience
The Queen Elizabeth Hall, London	Greater London	■				■		
The Purcell Room, London	Greater London	■					■	
The Waterfront, Norwich	Eastern		■			■		Live music/drama-share
Nottingham Concert Hall	East Midlands	■			■			Linked to theatre
The Maltings Concert Hall, Snape	Eastern		■			■		
University of Warwick Arts Centre	West Midlands	■			■			Part of University Arts complex
The Countess of Huntingdon's Hall, Worcester	West Midlands		■			■		Virtually self-financing

MULTI-PURPOSE

Building	Region	New Building	Conversion	Improvement/Refurbishment	Large	Medium	Small	Special Features
Wilde Theatre, South Hill Park, Bracknell	Southern	■				■		Dance studio
Minerva Studio Theatre, Chichester	Southern	■				■		Building incudes club & large rest.
Christ's Hospital Arts Centre, Horsham	Southern	■				■		Adaptable school facility
Derngate Centre, Northampton	East Midlands	■			■			Highly adaptable main space
Albany Empire, Deptford, London	Greater London	■				■		Mixed arts & community use
Edward Alleyn Hall, Dulwich College, London	Greater London	■					■	School facility
Almeida Theatre, Islington, London	Greater London		■				■	
Theatre Royal, Plymouth	South West	■			■			Theatre/concert hall

VISUAL ARTS, MEDIA AND CRAFTS BUILDINGS

Building	Region	New Building	Conversion	Improvement/Refurbishment	Large	Medium	Small	Special Features
Peacock Printmakers, Aberdeen	Scotland		■				■	Low cost studio/exhibition area
National Museum of Photo., Film & Television, Bradford	Yorkshire		■		■			
The Cambridge Darkroom	Eastern		■				■	
Edinburgh City Arts Centre	Scotland		■		■			
Pearoom Centre for Contemporary Crafts, Heckington	Lincolnshire & Humberside		■				■	Rural craft initiative
Ferens Art Gallery Extension, Hull	Lincolnshire & Humberside	■				■		Planning gain scheme
European Visual Arts Centre, Ipswich	Eastern	■				■		
Tate Gallery, Liverpool	Merseyside		■			■		Urban regeneration initiative
Greenwich Community Cinema, London	Greater London	■					■	Local authority/commercial initiative
Whitechapel Art Gallery, London	Greater London			■			■	
Cornerhouse, Manchester	North West		■			■		Wide activity range
Nottingham Community Arts	East Midlands		■				■	Multi-cultural project
Light House Media Centre, Wolverhampton	West Midlands		■			■		Wide mix of uses

ARTS CENTRES AND MIXED USE BUILDINGS

Building	Region	New Building	Conversion	Improvement/Refurbishment	Large	Medium	Small	Special Features
Watermans Arts Centre, Brentford	Greater London	■				■		Planning gain scheme
The Mechanics Institute, Burnley	North West		■		■			Arts/Entertainment/Community mix
Corn Exchange, Cambridge	Eastern		■		■			Arts/Ent. mix Concert hall standard
The Sands Centre, Carlisle	Northern	■			■			Sports/Arts/Leisure complex
Trinity Centre, Gainsborough	Lincolnshire & Humberside		■			■		
Queen's Hall, Hexham	Northern		■			■		Arts/Lib./Teach.ctr.mix serv.rural area
Horsham Arts Centre	Southern		■			■		Converted cinema
Phoenix Arts Centre, Leicester	East Midlands			■	■			Planning gain scheme
Nia Centre, Manchester	North West		■		■			Black Arts Centre
Newcastle Arts Centre	Northern		■		■			Includes range of commercial uses
The Leadmill, Sheffield	Yorkshire	■				■		
Trinity Arts Centre, Tunbridge Wells	South East		■				■	Low cost 'self-help' project
University of Warwick Arts Centre	West Midlands	■			■			Uni. Arts complx prov. facility for area
Windsor Community Arts Centre	Southern		■				■	Planning gain scheme

This list of buildings is included to provide points of reference, contacts and examples. The criteria for selection are as follows:

- buildings which offer interesting design solutions

- buildings which provide for the arts in new ways or with an interesting mix of uses

- buildings which demonstrate innovative approaches to the financing of new facilities

The selection aims to cover new buildings, conversions, refurbishments and improvements; large and small scale; a range of owners; a wide geographical spread.

Not all the buildings listed are successful in every respect but they each have some points of interest for other projects.

In the following text, the buildings are listed by region.

EASTERN ARTS

WOLSEY THEATRE
CIVIC DRIVE, IPSWICH, SUFFOLK
Completed in 1979, the Wolsey Theatre comprises an auditorium seating 440 people and a permanent operating base for a regional repertory company. The auditorium has an open stage with steeply raked seating in a fan shape. The side galleries can be used by either audience or performers and can be extended to wrap round the back of the stage. There is no fly tower but there are means of suspension over the stage operated from a top gallery also used for lighting. The ground floor entrance foyer has the box office and a coffee bar and the first floor houses the main theatre bar.
Architect: Roderick Ham and Partners
Theatre Consultant: Carr and Angier

EUROPEAN VISUAL ARTS CENTRE
IPSWICH
Scheduled to open in 1993 in the Ipswich Wet Dock, the European Visual Arts Centre plans to provide gallery and exhibition space, a visual arts information centre, lecture and seminar space, education facilities, a creche, a restaurant and arts related shops. Its exhibition programme will concentrate on historic and contemporary landscape art and on new art from throughout Europe. It is to be funded by a consortium of Ipswich Borough Council, the Arts Council, Eastern Arts, Suffolk County Council, the English Tourist Board and business interests. Regarded as an innovative venture in the visual arts in combining exhibitions with interactive public access information about art and its contexts, it could act as a prototype for other major arts developments.
Architect: To be the subject of a European Architectural Competition (1990)
Arts Consultant: Jeremy Rees

THE MALTINGS CONCERT HALL
SNAPE, SUFFOLK
Converted in 1967, Snape Maltings provides an attractive venue for concerts and recitals. While much of the original industrial character of the building is maintained, the extent of the conversion is far greater than it appears. For example, the authentic looking roof is new and new smoke hoods are used to house the dampers of the mechanical ventilation system. The acoustics of the main space are considered to be excellent for a range of concert performances.
Architects + Engineers + Quantity Surveyors: Arup Associates

THE CAMBRIDGE DARKROOM
DALES BREWERY, GWYDIR STREET, CAMBRIDGE
This is a simple but well designed facility providing a small photographic gallery and darkrooms for professional and local community use. It is an example of how thoughtful planning and design detailing can produce an attractive venue converted from a light industrial unit.
Architect: Owers and Lumley
Arts Consultant: Chris Baldwin ACT Consultant Services

CORN EXCHANGE
CAMBRIDGE
The Corn Exchange occupies an attractive building in the centre of Cambridge. Converted to its present use in 1986, it now houses a multi-purpose, local authority managed venue presenting a mixed programme of music (classical and rock), entertainment, exhibitions and conferences. It is generally thought to be a successful conversion, providing a good concert facility for the surrounding area combined with a venue for a wide range of arts, leisure and community uses. (Maximum seating capacity 1450.)
Architect: Arup Associates
(Illustrated on page 42)

NEW TOWNGATE THEATRE
BASILDON
Opened in 1988, this is a regional touring theatre (seating capacity 530) with a studio attached. The main auditorium offers a flexible space, based on a traditional design. It accommodates a full programme of touring, residences, studio and community work and provides a base for a touring company (Second Stride).
Architect: Renton Howard Wood Levin Partnership
Theatre Consultant: Technical Planning Ltd.

THE JUNCTION
CLIFTON ROAD, CAMBRIDGE
This is a new building designed to accommodate a range of arts and entertainment activities for young people. The single main space has a removable stage and retractable seating. The space is octagonal, enabling a range of layouts including a flat-floored arena, a wide fan (with the stage against one of the walls of the octagon) and an 'in the round' format. Additional facilities include bar and back-stage accommodation. A rehearsal space is planned to be incorporated in

due course. Particular attention has been given to sound insulation.
Architect: Cambridge City Council Architect's Department

THE WATERFRONT
10 BLACKFRIARS STREET, NORWICH
Scheduled to open at the end of 1990, the Waterfront is a live music and performance venue housed in a converted brewery warehouse on the banks of the river Wensum. It is the result of a five year campaign led by a group of young people seeking to provide a venue for music in the city. The Waterfront building comprises a 600 seat main space with a 120 seat studio as well as 2 cafe/bars and 3 rehearsal spaces. It is funded by Norwich City Council, in co-operation with the University of East Anglia, charitable trusts and the business community.
Architect: Norwich City Council Architect's Department

EAST MIDLANDS ARTS

THEATRE ROYAL AND CONCERT HALL
THEATRE SQUARE, NOTTINGHAM
The Theatre Royal is the main touring theatre for the East Midlands. Built in 1865, it was totally refurbished at the end of the 1970s. The existing auditorium was retained, as was the impressive front facade of the theatre but the stage and backstage areas were rebuilt so that large scale touring productions could be accommodated. The front of the house was also altered to provide more spacious foyer and bar areas. The theatre has a seating capacity of 1,138 which is regarded as somewhat low for a major touring venue.

Adjacent to the Theatre Royal and forming part of the same building complex, is the Royal Concert Hall. Opened in 1982, it is of an uncompromisingly modern design which is carefully related to the historic theatre building. Some of the backstage and the get-in areas are linked. The hall is designed to an international concert standard and also offers facilities for conference use.
(The Concert Hall seats 2,500.)
Architect: Renton Howard Wood Levin Partnership Theatre Consultant: Theatre Projects Ltd.
(Illustrated on page 76)

DERNGATE CENTRE
19/21 GUILDHALL ROAD, NORTHAMPTON
Opened in 1983, the Derngate Centre remains the best example in this country of a purpose built multi-use arts space. The main auditorium is a highly adaptable space in which an innovative system using pneumatic castors 'float' the large towers and blocks of seating from one position to another. The flexibility of layout and scale which this system offers, enables the main auditorium to accommodate a range of arts product as well as conferences, exhibitions, sports events and other leisure and entertainment activities. The building also provides space for a range of other arts, social and commercial activities.

The Centre has a seating capacity of 1,500 in its concert hall layout and accommodates 1,100 when used as a theatre. It has 1,000 sq.m. of exhibition space. The building was funded and is managed by the local authority.

The Centre is located close to the nineteenth century Theatre Royal, a traditional style theatre housing a repertory theatre, which provides a complementary facility.
Architect: Renton Howard Wood Levin Partnership Theatre Consultant: Theatre Projects Ltd.
(Illustrated on page 86)

NOTTINGHAM COMMUNITY ARTS
39 GREGORY BOULEVARD, HYSON GREEN NOTTINGHAM
Administered by an ethnically mixed professional team, the Nottingham Community Arts project occupies a former dispensary which has been imaginatively converted to provide facilities for photographic, print, art and craft work.
Architect: Alan Joyce - Extension Work Worker Team

PHOENIX ARTS CENTRE
11 NEWARKE STREET, LEICESTER
The Phoenix Theatre was originally constructed in the 1960s as a temporary facility to house productions while the Leicester Haymarket was being built. Popular demand caused its life to be extended but little was spent on improvement and maintenance. The development of a six storey car park immediately adjacent to its main entrance provided a reason and offered an opportunity (through planning gain) for improvements to be made.

A new entrance and facade has been built on what was originally the side door and elevation, which provides an extended foyer area and a café restaurant. The existing auditorium, foyer, box office, bar and kitchen have all been reorganised and refurbished. The project was a joint venture between Leicester City Council and Leicester Polytechnic.
Architect: Burrell Foley Associates
(Illustrated on page 66)

GREATER LONDON ARTS

EDWARD ALLEYN HALL, DULWICH COLLEGE
Completed in 1981, this is a purpose-built school theatre seating up to 290. A rectangular galleried auditorium with bleacher seating and a variable pit area in the floor permits a variety of stage layouts to be achieved or a completely flat floor created for non-theatrical events.
Architect: Tim Foster
(Illustrated on page 37)

WATERMANS ARTS CENTRE
40 HIGH STREET, BRENTFORD, MIDDLESEX
This is an example of a project which was the result of co-operation between a local authority and a developer. A substantial part of the cost of the building was met by the developer who built commercial office space on the rest of the site.

The Centre has a theatre, cinema, gallery and rehearsal facilities and a restaurant/bar/foyer area in which events such as jazz concerts are held.

The facilities for the disabled users are generally thought to be good. It opened in 1984.
Architect: Oscar Garry and Partners
Theatre/Arts Consultant: Carr and Angier
(Illustrated on pages 33 and 84)

THE QUEEN ELIZABETH HALL AND PURCELL ROOM
SOUTH BANK, LONDON
The Queen Elizabeth Hall and the Purcell Room are among the very few purpose-built halls for middle scale and small scale concerts in this country. Designed in 1967 as part of the South Bank arts complex, the halls form a single unit with a shared entrance and front of house facilities. In recent years the Queen Elizabeth Hall has been developed and the stage area extended to enable a wider range of productions, including opera and dance events, to be accommodated. (The Queen Elizabeth Hall seats 1065 and the Purcell Room seats 368.)
Architect: Greater London Council Architects Department

ALBANY EMPIRE
DOUGLAS WAY, DEPTFORD, LONDON SE18
The Albany building houses a mix of arts, community and social welfare activities, in a carefully planned and well designed building which aims to integrate the different interests of the organisation. There are two theatres within the complex, a small studio theatre and a larger space which can be used in a number of different forms.
(The main theatre space accommodates 150 and the studio space accommodates 80.)
Architect: Howell Killick Partridge and Amis

ALMEIDA THEATRE
ALMEIDA STREET, ISLINGTON, LONDON N1
The Almeida Theatre is housed in a former Scientific and Literary Institute which was converted into a Salvation Army Citadel around the turn of the of the century, when it was radically transformed with the insertion of cast iron gallery space and a new floor at ground level. The semi-circular interior layout reflects these former uses. The theatre provides a venue for a wide range of work from Europe, much of it of an innovative nature. Drama, dance, music (classical, contemporary and jazz) and mime have all been accommodated successfully in the theatre. The conversion work, which was funded from a variety of sources, was carried out in phases as money became available.
(The theatre seats 300.)
Architect:Burrell Foley

GREENWICH COMMUNITY CINEMA
180 GREENWICH HIGH ROAD, GREENWICH
The new cinema building forms part of the redevelopment of Burney Street, which includes housing, a hotel and an antique market. The project is a joint venture between the London Borough of Greenwich and a private cinema operator, Film Network. The local authority see the cinema as providing a focus for the whole community and plan to mount Saturday children's shows, multicultural films and events linked to the Greenwich Festival. As well as three auditoria (the largest seating 352 and the smallest seating 144) the building includes a range of café/bars as well as meeting areas. An innovative funding deal, involving a series of leases and sub-leases, means that both the local authority and the private operator stand to benefit financially. The cinema opened at the end of 1989.
Architect: Fletcher Priest

WHITECHAPEL ART GALLERY
80 WHITECHAPEL HIGH STREET, LONDON E1
The original gallery, a listed building, has undergone a major refurbishment and development programme to improve the environmental and security controls in the main exhibition areas, to offer better facilities for the public and to provide additional areas for education work. The refurbishment work has been carried out to a high standard to provide good technical and working conditions in line with current standards without compromising the quality of the existing building. An extension to the existing building houses a new gallery, new public staircases, café, education room, and lecture theatre as well as workshops and storage areas.
Architect: Colquhoun, Miller and Partners
(Illustrated on page 78)

TRICYCLE THEATRE
269 KILBURN HIGH ROAD, LONDON NW6
This 220 seat professional theatre was originally converted from a 1920s dance hall in 1980. Destroyed by fire in 1987, the building has now been rebuilt and extended. The auditorium consists of a two tier galleried courtyard constructed from a steel scaffolding system. The front-of-house areas provide a bar, gallery, community room and administrative offices.
Architect: Tim Foster
Theatre/Arts Consultant: Theatre Projects Ltd.

LINCOLNSHIRE AND HUMBERSIDE ARTS

TRINITY CENTRE
TRINITY STREET, GAINSBOROUGH, LINCOLNSHIRE
Opened in 1983, the Trinity Centre provides a performance space and support facilities within the interior of a Victorian church. It is a successful example of the re-use of a difficult type of building - the church follows the standard cruciform layout of the period and has a strong formal structure and appearance. The new centre takes advantage of the quality of the materials used in the original building but manages to soften and brighten the interior by careful choice of fittings. It is used for dance, drama and music productions as well as workshops and less formal events. It serves as a cinema which has become a significant source of revenue in support of other arts activities. The Centre is also a base for a successful team of outreach workers who operate throughout the scattered rural communities of West Lindsey District.
(The seating capacity of the auditorium is 200.)
Architect: Tim Benton
(Illustrated on page 19)

SPRING STREET THEATRE
HULL

The theatre is housed in a converted church hall and provides a working and performance base for the Hull Truck Theatre Company (a touring theatre group). The original conversion was undertaken in 1970 but further work has been carried out recently to provide better conditions. This refurbishment programme has provided an attractive venue at a relatively low cost. In addition to the production and performance work, the Spring Street Theatre provides workshops, music, educational activities and youth theatre. (The seating capacity of the auditorium is 200.) (Note: The rapid expansion and national success of the Company is leading Hull Truck, the City Council and the Regional Arts Association to look for planning-gain opportunities to provide the Company with a larger base and the City with a medium-sale auditorium.)
Architect: ABC Architects

FERENS ART GALLERY EXTENSION
PRINCE'S DOCK, HULL

Scheduled to open in 1991, the Ferens Art Gallery Extension is an example of 'planning gain'. Hull City Council entered into negotiations with various developers about proposals for a shopping development on the site of the former Prince's Dock, adjacent to the existing Art Gallery. The provision of an extension to the Gallery was made a condition of planning consent.

Land Securities is developing the whole of the Prince's Dock area, and Balfour Beatty are constructing a very large shopping centre set on concrete stilts above the water of the dock itself. Adjacent to it on the Dockside, this major extension to the Ferens Art Gallery will provide some 573 square metres of additional exhibition space to accommodate national and international exhibitions, capitalising on Hull's growing links with Europe.
Architect: Hugh Martin Partnership

PEAROOM CENTRE FOR CONTEMPORARY CRAFTS
HECKINGTON, SLEAFORD, LINCOLNSHIRE

A converted pea processing warehouse, a Victorian agricultural building of some character, now houses a large regional crafts centre. The centre is run by North Kesteven District Council, an authority which is regarded as having an innovatory approach to arts provision in rural areas, in a partnership with local heritage trust, the Regional Arts Association and local business interests.
Architect: Arthur Ling Associates

MERSEYSIDE ARTS

TATE GALLERY, LIVERPOOL
ALBERT DOCK, LIVERPOOL

The Tate Gallery is housed in a converted warehouse, originally built in 1846, in the north west corner of the Albert Dock. The seven storey building provides a series of galleries designed for 20th century art, artists studios, a performance space, a public reading room, classroom, restaurant and bookshop. The conversion has been carried out with as few alterations to the original building as possible. The major adjustment to the interior was the inclusion of a service core containing staircases, lifts and service ducts. Temperature and humidity controls in the galleries are achieved through a system of continuous ducting suspended below the existing vaulted ceilings.
Architect: Stirling Wilford and Associates
Arts Consultant: Richard Francis
(Illustrated on page 78)

NORTHERN ARTS

THE SANDS CENTRE
CARLISLE, CUMBRIA

The Centre, which is run by Carlisle City Council, is situated in the centre of the city in a parkland setting on the banks of the River Eden. It provides facilities for the city as well as for the large surrounding rural area on both sides of the border. The Centre offers a range of sports and leisure activities as well as providing space for conferences and exhibitions. It also mounts a full arts programme, including a season of symphony concerts, the Royal Shakespeare Company's touring productions and Opera 80 productions. The main hall, which can accommodate 1,400 people, is designed as a flexible space providing raked seating in a number of formats. It is technically equipped for a range of arts uses and has reasonable backstage facilities. The complex includes a smaller hall, a function suite, a restaurant seating up to 500 people and a health and fitness suite.

In 1989 the centre won a Sports Council award for the range and quality of the provision it offers.
Architect: Carlisle City Council Architect's Department
(Illustrated on page 89)

QUEEN'S HALL
BEAUMONT STREET, HEXHAM, NORTHUMBERLAND

The Queen's Hall Centre occupies an attractive group of buildings in the centre of the town. Formerly the Town Hall and Corn Exchange, the buildings have been converted to provide the central library, a range of arts facilities and a teachers' centre within the one complex, with the shared use of many of the facilities. By combining activities in this way, the local authorities have made provision for a wide range of events to be presented to a high standard for the surrounding, predominantly rural, community. In addition to promoting visiting drama, dance and music companies, the Centre also undertakes educational activities, shows films and runs workshops. (The main auditorium has a seating capacity of 400 and the Library Theatre seats 150.)
Architect: Northumberland County Council Architect's Department
Theatre Consultant: Andre Tammes

NEWCASTLE ARTS CENTRE.
WESTGATE ROAD, NEWCASTLE

Occupying a large city centre site near the main station, Newcastle Arts Centre provides training facilities in crafts and video, retail outlets for local

craftsmen and workshops for craft based activities. The organisation took over a semi-derelict group of buildings and, funded by Newcastle City Council and Manpower Services Commission, refurbished and converted the area. As MSC funded labour is no longer available, this project cannot be used as a prototype for similar ventures but it does illustrate how the arts can be used to regenerate an area and how a mix of activities can operate.
Architect: Jane and David Darbyshire

THE THEATRE ROYAL
GREY STREET, NEWCASTLE
The Theatre Royal is a grade II* listed building with an impressive classical facade occupying a prominent position in one of Newcastle's main streets. It has recently been refurbished and extended to provide improved stage and back-stage facilities, to rationalise and extend the entrances and foyer space and to increase provision for performers. Some adjacent properties were acquired to provide the necessary additional space.
(The theatre seats 1,322.)
Architect: Renton Howard Wood Levin Partnership

NORTH WEST ARTS

ROYAL EXCHANGE THEATRE
ST ANN'S SQUARE, MANCHESTER
Opened in 1974, the Royal Exchange Theatre still provides a 'prototype' solution to the problems of putting a theatre into a large shell space. It is installed within the massive, impressive three-domed hall formerly used as a cotton exchange. The theatre is designed as an independent module, inserted into the great hall, with the space around used for circulation, foyers and front-of-house facilities. The glass-clad module contains seating for 750 people on three levels in a seven sided 'in the round' format, with all the associated theatre sound and lighting systems, counter-weights for flying light objects over the stage, and a variable acoustic achieved by incorporating or isolating the long reverberation time of the hall. A café, bar, restaurant and all back stage ancillary accommodation are housed in converted space surrounding the main hall.
Architect: Levitt Bernstein Associates Limited
Theatre Consultant: (Design) Richard Negri
(Technical) Theatre Projects Consultants
Acoustician: DK Jones

PALACE THEATRE
OXFORD STREET, MANCHESTER
This grade II listed late Victorian Theatre underwent a major refurbishment programme in 1979/80 improving both back-stage and audience facilities. Since then the theatre has become more economically viable and has led to other arts related initiatives which have all contributed to the regeneration of the surrounding area.
Architect: Smith and Way

CORNERHOUSE
70 OXFORD STREET, MANCHESTER
The Cornerhouse is a visual arts centre, housed in a converted furniture showroom and store on a

prominent corner site overlooking the Manchester Palace Theatre. It is spread over six floors in which are accommodated three cinemas, three exhibition galleries, education room, video store, bookshop, bar, cafe and box office. It shows exhibitions of painting, drawing, sculpture, photography, craft, architecture and design, and has a regular programme of films, video and television work with seminars, courses and practical sessions. Built and funded by a consortium of local authorities, public bodies (including the Arts Council and the British Film Institute) and commercial organisations, it can be regarded as a prototype for future media centre developments.
Architect: The Millard Design Partnership with Fletcher Priest
Arts Consultant: Dewi Lewis
(Illustrated on page 42)

NIA CENTRE
CHICHESTER ROAD, HULME, MANCHESTER
The Nia Centre (the word Nia is an African word meaning 'purpose') plans to provide a professionally equipped and resourced centre to cater for the growing interest in all forms of Black arts and culture. It is to be housed in the former BBC Playhouse Theatre, a grade II listed building, which is being converted to provide an adaptable performance space and facilities for a wide range of social and interactive activities. The project is being financed by Manchester City Council (Urban Programme), supported by a fundraising programme. It is planned to open late 1990/early 1991.
Architect: Mills Beaumont Leavey/Tim Ronalds
Sound and Light Consultants: Eammon Hunt/ Nicholas Pearson
Acoustics: Paul Gillieron
(Illustrated on page 13)

BURNLEY MECHANICS
MANCHESTER ROAD, BURNLEY
Opened in 1986, the Mechanics Institute comprises a range of adaptable spaces, designed to provide much needed arts and entertainment facilities for Burnley and the surrounding area. It is a local authority run facility, housed in a converted building of considerable historic interest (Listed grade II*). The main auditorium has a fixed stage and retractable seating so that the area can be used as a flat-floored space. There are several smaller performance/studio spaces as well as a cinema, gallery and bar. The building also houses the Tourist Information Centre and the Mid-Pennine Arts Association. The refurbishment and conversion work was funded by the local authority with the support of the Arts Council, the English Tourist Board and the Historic Buildings Council.
Architect: Burnley Borough Architect's Department
Theatre Consultant: Graham Walme

SOUTHERN ARTS

WILDE THEATRE
SOUTH HILL PARK, BRACKNELL
The Wilde Theatre was built in two phases, the first was completed in 1984 and the second in 1989. Phase I provides a performance space for

South Hill Park, one of the largest arts centres in the country: Phase II adds an art gallery and dance studio. The arts centre is housed in a converted manor house which has a number of small and medium scale rooms but no large performance space (its original theatre seated 80 people). Fortunately, the manor's extensive grounds remained with the arts centre which meant that there was more than adequate room to build additional facilities.

The arts centre has developed strong interests in music and small scale opera over the years so the new auditorium is designed on the 'courtyard' principle to accommodate both music and drama productions, with a variety of options possible for forestage, orchestra pit, and stalls seating arrangements.
(The theatre seats 350-400.)
Architect: Levitt Bernstein Associates Ltd.
Theatre Consultant: Theatre Projects Ltd.
Acoustician: Dr Frank Fahy
(Illustrated on page 40)

HORSHAM ARTS CENTRE
NORTH STREET, HORSHAM, WEST SUSSEX
There are surprisingly few examples of cinemas being successfully converted for use as arts centres. Horsham is one. The new theatre, which is designed on a narrow fan layout, is inserted into one end of the old cinema auditorium. The remaining part of the old auditorium is sectioned off and divided to provide a much smaller cinema, foyer and exhibition space, restaurant, offices and public facilities accommodated over two floors. The stage area, which includes a modified fly tower, is an addition to the existing building. The Centre was opened in 1985. It provides for a range of activities, drama, dance, music, film, exhibitions and workshops.
(The main performance space seats 450 and the new studio cinema seats 126.)
Architect: Renton Howard Wood Levin Partnership
Theatre Consultant: Carr and Angier

ARTS CENTRE
CHRIST'S HOSPITAL SCHOOL, HORSHAM
Opened in 1974, this award winning scheme can still be regarded as one of the best designed arts buildings attached to a school. It provides facilities for a mixed programme of performances and arts events which are open to the public and is used as a performance and teaching space by the school. The auditorium is designed on the 'courtyard' principle which can be adapted to accommodate music, drama and dance.
(The theatre seats 400-600 depending on the use and layout.)
Architect: Howell Killick Partridge and Amis
Theatre/Arts Consultant: Theatre Projects Ltd.
(Illustrated on page 87)

WINDSOR COMMUNITY ARTS CENTRE
THE OLD COURT, ST LEONARD'S ROAD, WINDSOR, BERKSHIRE
This is an example of how a 'planning gain' deal can be used to help a small organisation. The arts centre is now based in a converted law court and police station building. When the police vacated the building, it reverted to the County, which sought to sell it for commercial or residential use. The arts group campaigned for its public use and convinced the local authorities of the viability of running an arts centre there. This led to agreement with the developers, Speyhawk (then based in the area) for the development of the police station as offices on the understanding that the law court would be converted into a base for the community arts group at the developer's expense. The arts group raised funds to fit out and equip the building. It was completed in 1981, and both the local authority and the developer remain closely involved, through a trust set up to oversee the use of the arts section of the building: a theatre/cinema (seating 190), general purpose studio, and cafe bar. A gallery was added in 1987. Speyhawk charge a rent of two magnums of champagne, which is delivered at an annual 'drinking the rent' ceremony.
Architect: Speyhawk (initial conversion) David Bishop and Clive Robinson (subsequent additions)

MINERVA STUDIO THEATRE
FESTIVAL THEATRE, CHICHESTER
Opened in 1989, the Minerva Studio Theatre provides additional facilities for the Chichester Festival Theatre. The new building houses a 255 seat auditorium, a large restaurant serving both theatres, a theatre shop and a clubroom and headquarters for the Festival Theatre Society. The foyer and restaurant areas are designed to take full advantage of the parkland setting.

The auditorium has a thrust stage and a flexible seating system which can be changed from a fan-shaped theatre layout to a modified end-stage format to enable the auditorium to be used as a cinema and as a conference venue.

The project was financed largely through donations and commercial sponsorship.
Architect: Kenzie Lovell
(Illustrated on page 40)

SOUTH EAST ARTS

TRINITY ARTS CENTRE
CHURCH ROAD, TUNBRIDGE WELLS
The Trinity Theatre and Arts Association was formed in 1974 by the Civic Society and Drama Club for the purpose of restoring the fabric of the redundant Holy Trinity Church, a Grade 1 listed building in the centre of Tunbridge Wells, converting it into an arts centre and running it. Restoration of the building began in 1979 and conversion in 1980, with the first events taking place in 1982. The Centre now provides a 275 seat theatre/concert hall with raked seating as well as exhibition galleries, meeting rooms and a spacious bar and buffet. A varied programme of drama, music, dance and exhibitions is mounted maintaining a policy of a 50/50 mix of professional and local amateur productions.

Trinity Arts Centre is run by 300-strong team of volunteers. There are several paid staff. The restoration and conversion work was carried out by volunteers with the help of the Keyscheme (Community Project) which supplied a small building team, and of the West Kent College

Construction Department.
Architect: D Joyce and later D Christmas
Theatre/Arts Consultant: Herbert Story

SOUTH WEST ARTS

THEATRE ROYAL
ROYAL PARADE, PLYMOUTH
The Theatre Royal which was completed in 1982
is designed to serve a range of functions. It is the
only major auditorium west of Bristol and as such
has to accommodate touring drama, opera and
dance companies and serve as a concert hall. It
also provides a base for the regional repertory
company. The theatre has a number of special
features which enable it to function in its triple
role. The seating capacity and scale of the
auditorium can be reduced by lowering the
ceiling to cut off the upper seating tier. This
makes it suitable for a wide range of drama
productions. 'Assisted resonance' - an electronic
sound control system which modifies the reverberation times - has been installed to adapt the
acoustics to the varying requirements of speech
and music.

The seating capacity of the auditorium when the
upper level is in use is 1296. This capacity is
reduced to 764 when the ceiling is lowered.

The building also contains a small studio theatre.
Architect: Peter Moro Partnership
Theatre Consultant: Carr and Angier
Acoustics Consultant: Sound Research
Laboratories Ltd.
(Illustrated on page 40)

THEATRE ROYAL
BEAUFORT SQUARE, BATH, AVON
Originally built in 1863, the grade II listed
Theatre Royal occupies a tight urban site in the
centre of Bath. A major refurbishment programme was carried out in the mid-1980's. The
stage, backstage and get-in improvements
enabled the theatre to promote a wider range of
touring product and the front of house improvements enabled it to increase its audience and its
earned income. The theatre is also able to take
advantage of the quality of its building and of the
position it occupies, to mount special events
which attract sponsorship and to hire out its
facilities for receptions and parties. These
initiatives, made possible by the refurbishment of
the building, have contributed to a marked
improvement in the financial viability of the
theatre.
Architect: Dowton & Hurst

WEST MIDLANDS ARTS

BIRMINGHAM HIPPODROME
HURST STREET, BIRMINGHAM
Originally built in 1899, it was substantially
improved and refurbished in 1980/1981, when
the theatre's ownership and operation came
under a charitable trust.

The Birmingham Hippodrome is one of the
largest theatres in the country seating 1943, and
the major touring venue for the West Midlands
with a large stage (42' opening and 57' depth)
complemented by excellent backstage facilities.
As from August 1990, the theatre is the homebase
for the Birmingham Royal Ballet (formerly
Sadler's Wells Royal Ballet) which has been attracted to Birmingham from London. The new
base accommodates four excellent rehearsal
studios, and all the company administration and
technical services, except scenery storage.
*Architect (1990): The Seymour Harris Partner-
ship, Birmingham*
Theatre Consultant: John Wyckham

LIGHT HOUSE MEDIA CENTRE
CENTRAL ART GALLERY, LICHFIELD STREET,
WOLVERHAMPTON
The Light House Media Centre was opened in
1987 as a result of a partnership between Wolverhampton Borough Council and Wolverhampton
Polytechnic. A 19th century Chubb Locks Works
is to be converted and extended to provide two
cinemas, exhibition spaces, conference facilities,
shop, cafe, a home for the Regional Media
Reference Library and the Arts Council's Video
Access Library for the West Midlands. All this is
housed in a joint private/public sector venture
which also contains bars and shops, together with
studios and offices to rent.
Architect: Robert Seager Design
Theatre Consultant: Fletcher Priest
Chris Ellicott

UNIVERSITY OF WARWICK ARTS CENTRE
COVENTRY
The Centre comprises a number of separate
facilities offering a high standard of provision for
drama, dance and music. The main buildings are
the theatre, the concert hall (which serves as the
main concert venue for the area), and the more
recently completed exhibition galleries. They
provide one of the most successful of the 'campus' based arts facilities in that they genuinely
serve both the University and the surrounding
area.

(The facilities comprise the main theatre auditorium seating 573; the Concert Hall seating 1517;
an Ensemble room seating 100; a Conference
Room seating 250; a studio theatre seating 200;
and three galleries offering 6,000 sq. ft. of exhibition space.)

Architect: Renton Howard Wood Levin Partnership
Theatre Consultant: (Theatre and Studio) Theatre
Projects Ltd.

THE COUNTESS OF HUNTINGDON'S
HALL
DEANSWAY, WORCESTER
The Hall is a listed building. It was built as a
chapel in 1773 and became redundant for that
purpose in 1976. Since then a preservation trust
has restored the structure and eighteenth
century interior of the building and converted it
for use as a concert hall and multi-purpose venue.
Opened in 1987, it is regarded as an excellent
venue for small scale concerts and recitals both
in terms of its acoustic quality and the pleasant
ambience it offers. It seats a maximum of 500.

Most of the funds required for the restoration were raised by donations, sponsorship and fundraising.
Architect: Buttress Fuller Geoffrey Alsop
(Illustrated on page 77)

NEW VICTORIA THEATRE
STOKE-ON-TRENT
Built in 1985, the New Victoria Theatre was designed to provide a new working base and performance venue for the Victoria Theatre Company. It was designed to a very exact brief, prepared by the Theatre Director, based on his experience of working with theatre in the round over many years. The auditorium forms the core of the building. The surrounding areas provide circulation and meeting places, exhibition space, bars and restaurant facilities.

Particular attention was given in the design to the quality of the working conditions provided for the performers and technical staff. The theatre is an attractive, domestically scaled building in a pleasantly landscaped setting, designed to conserve the natural environment.
(The seating capacity is 600 - the layout enables all the seats to be within 26' of the acting area.)
Architect:Hollins Jones Oldacre & Partners
Acoustics Consultant: Rupert Taylor
(Illustrated on page 83)

YORKSHIRE ARTS

ALHAMBRA THEATRE
GREAT HORTON ROAD/MORLEY STREET, BRADFORD
The Alhambra Theatre is a grade II listed building completed just before the first World War. It has recently been completely refurbished and extended to provide improved stage and backstage accommodation as well as more spacious facilities for the audience. The adjacent building houses a studio and rehearsal space. This city centre development is part of Bradford City Council's plans for improving the appearance, facilities and economic life of the Bradford area, through arts provision and through tourism. The Alhambra development was substantially funded by a grant from the EC's Social Fund.
(The Alhambra Theatre has a seating capacity of 1,500.)
Architect: Renton Howard Wood Levin Partnership
Theatre Consultant: Theatre Projects Ltd.

NATIONAL MUSEUM OF PHOTOGRAPHY, FILM AND TELEVISION,
PRINCES VIEW, BRADFORD
This is an example of a local authority using arts provision as a catalyst for urban renewal. The Museum is a regional extension of the Science Museum and funding for it was attracted to Bradford against competition from other authorities. It is housed in a converted theatre (an early and unsuccessful example of planning gain). The museum has the only IMAX cinema in the country (the picture is projected laterally onto a screen 52' high and 64' wide), conference facilities and an education unit in addition to galleries housing the permanent displays and changing exhibitions. In 1989, the Kodak Museum was added: 1,000 square metres of display space, adapted from an underground car park adjacent to the original building. In 1990 the top floor of the Museum was adapted to provide a transmitting television studio, acting as TV-am's regional station, and a lease was acquired on the adjacent library theatre, in order to convert the premises into a multi-purpose cinema.
Architect: Richard Seifert
Theatre/Arts Consultant: Bradford Metropolitan Architects Department/Richard Fowler

THE LEADMILL
6/7 LEADMILL ROAD, SHEFFIELD
The Leadmill provides a centre for touring theatre, dance, performance art, live bands, classical and contemporary music, jazz, cabaret and discos. Housed in a series of converted industrial buildings in the centre of Sheffield, it offers a wide range of popular entertainment and recreational activities as well as mounting an innovative programme of arts events. It is also involved in educational work. The converted mill buildings are designed to be approachable and relaxed. The layout of the main spaces is informal and adaptable.

Its success has led to its expanding into adjacent premises and to other arts oriented organisations moving into the area. What started as a fairly low key way of improving an area with MSC funding is now seen as an example of the use of the arts as a catalyst for the regeneration of rundown urban areas. The City Council has declared the whole area around the Leadmill as a Cultural Industries Quarter.
(The main space has a seating capacity of 600.)
Architect: Allen Todd

WEST YORKSHIRE PLAYHOUSE
QUARRY HILL MOUNT, LEEDS
The West Yorkshire Playhouse opened its new building in March 1990. Designed to replace the old Leeds Playhouse building which had come to the end of its lease on the University site, the new building provides more space and caters for a wider range of activities.

The building comprises a fan shaped auditorium with a modified flytower and a smaller more adaptable second performance space. As well as serving as a working and performing base for the resident company, it provides a venue for visiting groups. Particular attention has been given to accommodating the special requirements of dancers and dance companies.
(The seating capacity of the larger auditorium, The Quarry Theatre, is 750. The smaller auditorium, The Courtyard Theatre, seats 350.)
Architect: The Appleton Partnership
Theatre/Arts Consultant: Carr and Angier
Sandy Brown Associates (Acoustics)
(Illustrated on page 21)

SCOTLAND

DUNDEE REPERTORY THEATRE
TAY SQUARE, DUNDEE
This is a new theatre completed in April 1982 to house the existing Repertory Company. When it

was built it comprised an auditorium and stage with a flytower as well as most of the facilities needed by the producing company. Since that date, the company's activities have expanded considerably and the building has been extended to provide additional production facilities - a paint shop, scene dock storage, design studio and more wardrobe space. The extension also provides accommodation for the theatre's dance company and the community drama project, both of which have developed since the new building opened.

The theatre, which is adjacent to the University in a historic area in the centre of the city, is effectively fitted into a very tight site.
Architect: Nichol Russell Partnership
Theatre Consultant: Andre Tammes

QUEEN'S HALL
CLERK STREET, EDINBURGH
The Queen's Hall provides recital room/concert venue in a converted, listed parish church. The closing of the church coincided with the search for premises by two orchestras - the Scottish Baroque Ensemble and the Scottish Chamber Orchestra. They were joined in their search for an operating base and rehearsal facilities by the Scottish Philharmonic Singers. The church fulfilled these requirements as well as offering a new concert venue.

The conversion has maintained the quality and much of the actual structure of the existing building and made use of its naturally fine acoustics.
Architect: Robert Hurd and Partners
(Illustrated on page 42)

PEACOCK PRINTMAKERS
21 CASTLE STREET, ABERDEEN
The Peacock Printmakers are a group of artists occupying two adjacent converted buildings in the centre of Aberdeen. The buildings provide working studios, an exhibition space and sales area. This is a small scale project which has enabled a range of spaces to be provided for arts use at a relatively low cost.

CITIZENS THEATRE
GORBALS, GLASGOW
Since 1978, when the first phase of an extended programme of improvements was put in hand, the Citizens Theatre has been totally refurbished - the theatre had survived without any major repairs since it was built in 1878. Over the last decade the backstage areas have been improved, the auditorium and front-of-house has been extended and redecorated, new facilities have been added and the front facade has been rebuilt. The work has been funded by the Glasgow District Council, Strathclyde Regional Council, the Scottish Development Agency, the Scottish Arts Council and by the theatre itself.
Architect: Department of Architecture and Related Services of Glasgow District Council
Building Design Partnership (new frontage)

EDINBURGH CITY ART CENTRE
1-4 MARKET STREET, EDINBURGH
In 1981, Edinburgh's Art Centre moved into its new premises in an elegant newspaper warehouse building designed at the turn of the century. The exhibition galleries, which are spread over five floors, house the City's fine art collection and provide space for visiting exhibitions. They are serviced and equipped to international standards. The Centre includes full supporting facilities for the care and display of works of art as well as a café/bar and lecture room.
Architect: City of Edinburgh Architect's Department

PERTH THEATRE
HIGH STREET, PERTH
The repertory theatre has been extended and refurbished in two phases to improve facilities both for the productions and the audience. The first phase, which was completed in 1981, refurbished the auditorium, extended the workshop area and provided attractive new restaurant facilities. The second phase, completed in 1985, added new dressing rooms and a studio theatre.
Architect: Gordon & Dey Partnership
(Illustrated on pages 70 and 80 and 83)

WALES

GRAND THEATRE
SINGLETON STREET, SWANSEA
Swansea Grand Theatre was built in 1897. The original building had a very fine auditorium but, in common with many of the theatres of this period, very limited stage and backstage facilities and poor front of house conditions. It has now been totally refurbished with the area to the rear of the proscenium arch being substantially rebuilt to a modern design. This has enabled the theatre to promote a wider range of work including that produced by the major touring companies.
(The seating capacity is 1,100.)
Architect: Swansea City Council Director of Development
Theatre Consultant: Carr and Angier

This information is taken from 'Theatres - Planning Guidance for Design and Adaptation' edited by Roderick Ham (1987). It is reprinted here with the permission of the publishers Butterworth Architecture.

The legislation mentioned in this chapter is current in the United Kingdom at the time of writing. It is based on British experience in theatres, which is considerable, and many countries in the world now base their requirements on, for example, the GLC regulations.

Places of public entertainment in the United Kingdom are controlled under various enactments, some general and some locally applied. Under the Theatres Act, 1968, every house or other place of public resort kept for the public performance of stage plays must have either the authority of letters patent or a licence. Patent theatres were granted a royal charter by Charles II. They are the Theatre Royal, Drury Lane, the Royal Opera House, Covent Garden, and the Theatre Royal, Haymarket, all of them in London.

LICENSING AUTHORITIES
The county or county borough council has the authority to grant licences within its area, except that, by virtue of the Local Government Act, 1985, the entertainment licensing functions of the Greater London Council were transferred to the London borough councils and the Common Council (City of London), and those of metropolitan county councils were transferred to the metropolitan district councils.

A county council, other than those last mentioned, may delegate these powers to a district council.

FILM EXHIBITIONS
Under the Cinemas Act of 1985 a licence is required for all film exhibitions other than private film exhibitions. A licence is required whatever type of film is used, whether non-flammable or flammable, or video or other television equipment other than for normal BBC or ITA broadcasts.

If the premises are used only occasionally and exceptionally for showing films to a paying public (which means not more than on six days in a year) a licence is not needed, but the occupier must comply with the Secretary of State's regulations, which are the cinematograph Regulations of 1955 and 1958 (shortly to be updated). He must also give the local licensing authority at least seven days' notice before the film show is due to take place and must comply with any conditions they may impose under cinematograph regulations.

No licence is required if members of the public are not admitted or if they are allowed in free. Institutions and non-profit-making organisations can ask the public to pay to see an occasional film without a licence for the premises. They can obtain exemption from the Secretary of State, but only if the premises have not been used on more than three of the preceding seven days for a similar exhibition.

THE USE OF PREMISES FOR MUSIC, DANCING, SINGING, BOXING AND WRESTLING
These forms of public entertainment are controlled by authorities in a similar manner but not all under the same legislation. The Greater London Council had its own regulations, so do certain parts of the Home counties. The rest of England and Wales is different again.

TECHNICAL REQUIREMENTS, REGULATIONS AND RULES OF MANAGEMENT
The licensing authorities have power to make regulations affecting the construction and equipment of buildings used for public entertainment, particularly on matters of protection from fire. They may also make rules and conditions which must be observed by the occupiers to ensure that the premises are maintained in a safe condition. Some authorities issue their regulations and rules of management separately, while others combine them in one document.

THE HOME OFFICE MANUAL
The Secretary of State makes regulations for cinemas but not for other places of public entertainment. The Home Office Manual of Safety Requirements in Theatres and Other Places of Public Entertainment was issued in 1934 as a model code of requirements and conditions for the guidance of licensing authorities who would then make their own rules. Though it is rather out of date it still makes interesting reading and explains some of the background experience which led to the safety measures it recommends. It will be superseded by British Standard 5588: Part 6, Places of Assembly, which at the time of writing is in draft form.

THE GREATER LONDON COUNCIL REGULATIONS AND RULES
Up to the time of its abolition in 1986 the GLC had many more theatres within its area than any other licensing authority in the United Kingdom and its regulations for places of public entertainment in London were comprehensive, covering the site, general arrangements, construction, electrical and mechanical services, lighting, heating and ventilation. It had a department with much experience of administering the regulations, and it was sufficiently flexible to take account of new techniques, materials, methods of construction and of changing trends within the theatre such as the desire for open stages. The GLC issued separate Rules of Management. The GLC, and before it the London County Council, the LCC, were widely respected for the way in which they administered the licensing of theatres and their standards have been adopted elsewhere in the UK and in other countries. London is in for a time of great change, and it remains to be seen what effect the passing of responsibility for licensing control to the London boroughs has on London's Theatreland.

OTHER AUTHORITIES
Many authorities have based their regulations and rules on the Home Office manual, while others use those of the GLC as a basis. This variation from place to place makes it essential to

find out the particular local authority's requirements at an early stage in the design of any place of public entertainment.

THE FIRE PRECAUTIONS ACT, 1971
This Act will apply to theatres and various other places of assembly and resort, but the necessary designation order for this purpose has not yet been made. Its purpose is to strengthen and rationalise the law relating to fire precautions in these places and in hotels, boarding houses and similar residential premises and offices, shops, railway premises and factories, including "factories" in theatres. It was also designed to control some places which had so far escaped the net, such as club theatres. Occupiers of premises used for such purposes will, upon designation, have to obtain a certificate of approval of means of escape from the fire authority, to whom they will have to submit full particulars of the premises and its uses, including plans. The building will be inspected where necessary and any work which must be carried out will be notified. This will have to be completed before a fire certificate is issued. The requirements may include conditions about providing and maintaining means of escape, employing enough staff, and training them in what to do in case of fire. Records of fire drill and any incidents may have to be kept ready for inspection. If for a particular premises it is physically impossible to comply with the requirements, then the fire authority may for instance limit the number of people who may be accommodated.

Any offices, shops and "factories" (such as the workshop and backstage areas of some theatres) in places of entertainment are already designated under the Fire Precautions Act by virtue of the Fire Precautions (Factories, Offices, Shops and Railway Premises) Order, 1976, and fire certificates as described above may therefore be necessary in some cases. The fire authority will see that there are proper means of escape for the staff.

BUILDING AND OTHER REGULATIONS
ABOUT FIRE PRECAUTIONS
The fire certificate under the Fire Precautions Act, 1971, is needed by the occupiers of some existing buildings so that the fire authority can keep a check on their use. When it comes to new buildings, the Department of Environment has made building regulations concerning means of escape under the Building Act, 1984, and the Secretary of State has powers to amend local Acts such as the London Building Acts. He can make regulations to control means of escape, the internal construction of the building, and other matters which are dealt with during the life of the building by the fire certificate.

The Fire Precautions Act does not introduce any additional regulations to the provisions of the Cinemas Act, 1985, but this legislation comes under its wing and amendments may eventually be made.

OTHER GENERAL LEGISLATION
Theatres and other places of public entertainment are also subject to the various Acts which apply to most other types of building, such as: the Town and Country Planning Acts; the National Building Regulations, 1985, for England and Wales, which apply also to the Inner London Boroughs by virtue of the Secretary of State's regulations. In addition, in the Inner London Boroughs, the London Building Acts, 1930-1939, as amended by the Secretary of State's regulations, will apply.

The Health and Safety at Work Act, 1974, is equivalent to entertainment licensing regulations but applies at all times.

ACCESS FOR THE DISABLED
It should be noted that the National Building Regulations, 1985, require proper provision for disabled people. Buildings must comply with Regulation 4, Schedule 2, Facilities for Disabled People.

NOTE:
The Home Office has recently published a 'Guide to Fire Precautions in existing places of entertainment and like premises' (1990).

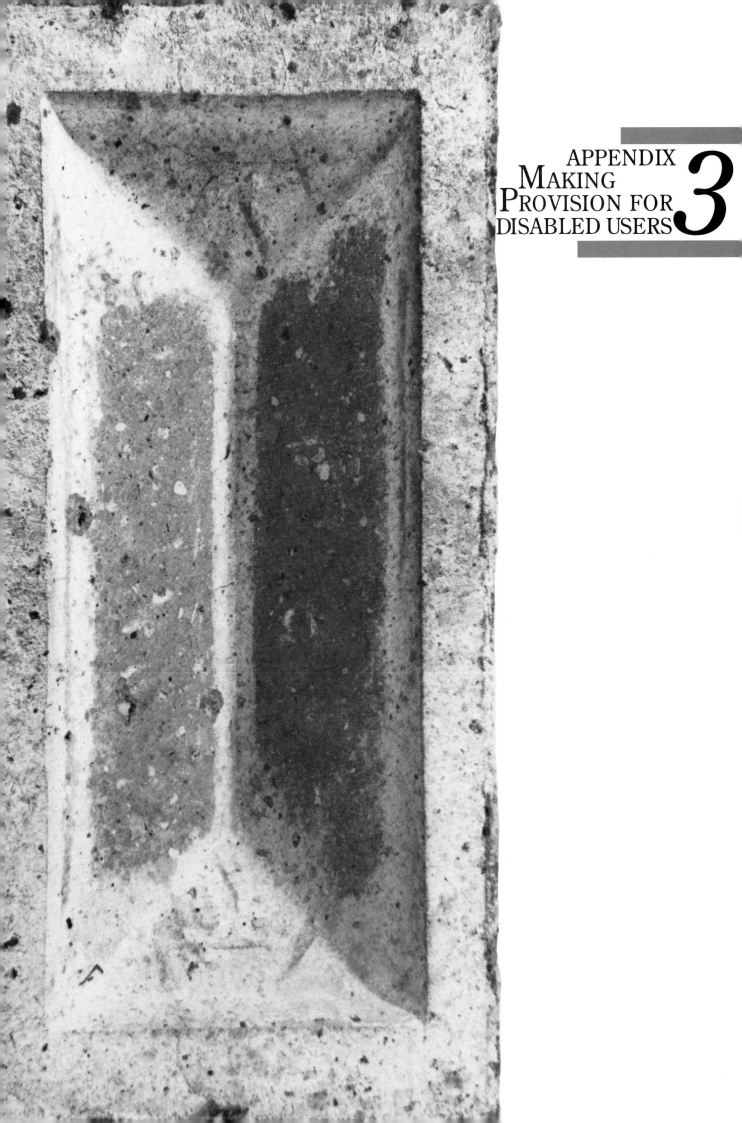

LEGISLATIVE REQUIREMENTS

There is a range of legislation relating to the provision of facilities to make buildings accessible to disabled people. This means, in effect, that those concerned with the provision of buildings for the arts are required by law to make them accessible to those with disabilities.

For example, Section 4 of the Chronically Sick and Disabled Person Act 1970 requires that 'any person undertaking the provision of any building or premises to which the public are to be admitted, whether on payment or otherwise, shall, in the means of access both to and within the premises, and in the parking facilities and sanitary conveniences to be available (if any), make provision for the needs of members of the public visiting the building or premises who are disabled'.

The Ministry of Housing and Local Government Circular 65/70 cites public halls, public libraries, theatres, cinemas and shops as 'obvious examples of buildings to which the public are to be admitted'. The circular confirms that 'provision' covers 'not only new construction but also conversion of existing buildings'.

There are also requirements concerning provision for people with disabilities included in the Building Regulations.

Legislation is continually being amended and updated so it is advisable to consult the specialist sources for information on detailed current legislation. (See below and in the bibliography.)

ARTS COUNCIL'S CODE OF PRACTICE

The Arts Council has drawn up a Code of Practice on Arts and Disability which it expects all those in receipt of subsidy to work towards implementing. This covers a much wider range of facilities, policies and attitudes than just making sure that buildings can be used by people with disabilities but access is an important part of it.

Copies of the Code are available from the Arts Council together with copies of the Arts and Disabilities Action Plan which makes recommendations for its implementation.

ADDITIONAL SOURCES OF INFORMATION

There is a good range of published material giving information on the provision and design of facilities for people with disabilities. 'Arts for Everyone: Guidance for Provision for Disabled People' by Anne Pearson, which contains drawings suggesting ways of adapting existing buildings, and the Arts Council's 'Arts and Disability Resource Pack' provide detailed information on what is required. The Museums and Galleries Commission is currently (mid-1990) producing an update brochure to 'Arts for Everyone' which lists and explains legislation introduced since 1986 when the original book was published. The Centre on Environment for the Handicapped, with the backing of the Royal Institute of British Architects, has set up an Architectural Advisory Service to provide information on local architects with experience in designing for the disabled.

INCREASING ACCESSIBILITY TO THE BUILDINGS

What follows is intended to give an indication of the range of provision to be considered and the areas requiring special attention. It is not a compete list of the problems, possible solutions and opportunities which exist. These are covered in detail in the specialist literature.

The term 'disabled' relates to a wide range of conditions affecting a significant proportion of the population. Those working in the field estimate that between 10% and 14% of the population have some form of disability. Wheelchair users account for about 10% of disabled people. Other disabilities which need to be recognised in the design of arts buildings and the provision of facilities for the arts include those who have difficulty in walking, the frail and elderly and those with impaired vision and hearing.

As a general principle, disabled people should be enabled to use a building and participate in the arts on the same basis as the more able bodied sections of the population (i.e. wherever possible, the normal routes, lifts, seating areas, entrances etc. should be designed so that they can be used by disabled people rather than providing special facilities which have the effect of separating those with some form of disability from the rest of the public).

This applies to all those who use a building - the public, performers and those who work in the building.

The following areas need to be given special consideration.

PARKING
Bays should be provided close to the appropriate access points (main entrance for the public, backstage entrance for performers) and clearly marked as reserved for use by disabled people.

RAMPS
Ramps are needed wherever there is a change of level to be negotiated. These should be no steeper than 1 in 12 and should have a non-slip surface and a handrail to help ambulant disabled people.

DOORS
Attention should be paid to the weight, the speed at which they close, the handles and grips (the height as well as the shape and ease of use). Revolving doors create a barrier for many disabled people.

CIRCULATION ROUTES
All routes should be wide enough for a wheelchair and provide adequate turning spaces. They should be equipped with handrails where possible and be kept clear.

LIFTS
Lifts should be large enough for a wheelchair, its occupant and a companion. Controls should be

within reach of wheelchair users and people of small stature. Braille markings and an auditory signal indicating floor levels are helpful for those with visual impairments.

Where lifts are to be used as a means of escape, specialist advice needs to be sought to ensure their safety in a fire or other emergency.

LAVATORIES
The toilet facilities need to be spacious, easily accessible and available for use by both sexes (so that a companion can accompany a disabled user). They should be provided with the appropriate grab rails.

SEATING
Opinions differ as to whether it is preferable to provide seating which a disabled person can use (transferring from a wheelchair which then needs to be stored in an accessible position) or whether to provide wheelchair spaces (thus separating disabled patrons from their companions). Where possible, it is probably better to offer the option of being part of the main audience to those who are able to transfer quite easily to the auditorium seating. Consideration should also be given to providing seats with sufficient space in front for ambulant disabled people and for those with guide dogs.

THE BOX OFFICE
This should be designed so that those in wheel-chairs and those of small stature can be seen by the staff. Where security demands glazing between the public and the staff, some means should be found of helping the hard of hearing to communicate.

TELEPHONES AND OTHER EQUIPMENT
These should be at a height which can be used by those in wheelchairs or those of small stature or special facilities should be provided and clearly marked.

SIGNS
All signs should be clear and easy to read. There are a series of symbols devised by the Access and Information Group which are generally under-stood by disabled people.

MEANS OF ESCAPE
It is important that disabled people should not only be given access to public buildings but that they should be able to get out of them quickly should the need arise. The local fire officer will advise on this aspect when considering the overall means of escape and may impose some restrictions on the number of wheelchair users who can be admitted to the building at any one time in order to safeguard the escape routes.

INCREASING PARTICIPATION IN THE ARTS
Making buildings as accessible as possible is only a small part of opening up arts buildings for the enjoyment of the disabled members of the public. Many of the problems related to the use of existing buildings can be overcome by good management, positive staff attitudes, and clear information in publicity.

The general requirements set out above should be related to the needs of members of staff, performers and artists and applied to the back-stage, studio, rehearsal, technical and office areas as well as to the spaces used by the public.

Some members of the public can be enabled to appreciate the arts more fully if facilities are made available for them to do so.

FACILITIES FOR PEOPLE WITH IMPAIRED HEARING
Where signers are hired (to communicate by means of signs), special arrangements will need to be made. These do not, however, affect the design of a building.

Induction loops enable those with some hearing ability and those with hearing aids to hear more easily. The system is relatively simple and cheap to install especially when a new facility is being built or an existing building converted. Hearing enhancement can also be achieved through the provision of an infra-red system.

FACILITIES FOR PEOPLE WITH VISUAL IMPAIRMENTS
Generally all signs should be clear and simple. Doors should be distinguishable from their surrounds, and their method of opening be made obvious. Large glazed doors and revolving doors represent potential hazards. Attention should be drawn to steps and changes of level.

Audio description is a method by which the visual element of a performance is described to the blind members of the audience. A soundproof box or room, with good sight of the stage is required. This is linked into the induction loop system.

APPENDIX
DIRECTORY **4**

ACRE (ACTION WITH COMMUNITIES IN
RURAL ENGLAND)
Stroud Road, Cirencester, Gloucester GL7 6JR
Tel: 0285 653477

ARCHITECTS REGISTRATION COUNCIL OF
THE UNITED KINGDOM (ARCUK),
73 Hallam Street, London W1N 6EE
Tel: 071 580 5861

ARCHITECTURAL HERITAGE FUND
17 Carlton House Terrace, London SW1Y 5AW
Tel: 071 925 0199

ARTS COUNCIL OF GREAT BRITAIN
14 Great Peter Street, London SW1P 3NQ
Tel: 071 333 0100

ARTS DEVELOPMENT ASSOCIATION
The Arts Centre, Vane Terrace, Darlington,
County Durham DL3 7AX
Tel: 0325 465930

ASSOCIATION FOR BUSINESS SPONSORSHIP
OF THE ARTS
Nutmeg House, 60 Gainsford Street,
Butlers Wharf, London SE1 2NY
Tel: 071 378 8143

ASSOCIATION OF COUNTY COUNCILS
Eaton House, 66A Eaton Square,
London SW1W 9BH
Tel: 071 235 1200

ASSOCIATION OF BRITISH THEATRE
TECHNICIANS (ABTT)
4 Great Pulteney Street, London W1R 3FD
Tel: 071 434 3901

ASSOCIATION OF COMMUNITY TECHNICAL
AID CENTRES Ltd.
Royal Institution, Colquitt Street,
Liverpool L1 4DE
Tel: 051 708 7607

ASSOCIATION OF DISTRICT COUNCILS
Chapter House, Chapter Street,
London SW1P 4ND
Tel: 071 233 6868

BRITISH FILM INSTITUTE
21 Stephen Street, London W1P 1PI.
Tel: 071 255 1444

CENTRE ON ENVIRONMENT FOR THE
HANDICAPPED
35 Great Smith Street, London SW1P 3BJ
Tel: 071 222 7980

BUSINESS IN THE COMMUNITY
227a City Road, London EC1V 1LX
Tel: 071 253 3716

CHARITIES AID FOUNDATION
48 Pembury Road, Tonbridge, Kent TN9 2JD
Tel: 0732 771 333

CHARITY COMMISSION
St Alban's House, 57- 60 Haymarket, London SW1
Tel: 071 210 3000

COMMISSION FOR RACIAL EQUALITY
Elliot House, 10 -12 Allington Street,
London SW1E 5EH
Tel: 071 828 7022

CRAFTS COUNCIL
1 Oxendon Street, London SW1Y 4HT
Tel: 071 931 4811

DIRECTORY OF SOCIAL CHANGE
Radius Works, Back Lane, London NW3 1HL
Tel: 071 431 1817

ENGLISH HERITAGE
23 Savile Row, London W1X 1AB
Tel: 071 937 3000

ENGLISH TOURIST BOARD
Grants and Development Department
Thames Tower, Blacks Road,
Hammersmith W6 9EL
(written enquiries only)

EUROPEAN COMMUNITY (EC)
European Social Fund Unit,
Department of Employment, 11 Belgrave Road,
London SW1V 1RB
Tel: 071 834 6644

HMSO BOOKSHOP
PO Box 276, 51 Nine Elms Lane,
London SW8 5DT
Tel: 071 873 0011

INSTITUTE OF ACOUSTICS
PO Box P320, ST Albans, Herts HL1 1P2
Tel:0727 48195

INSTITUTE OF CHARITY FUNDRAISING
MANAGERS
208/210 Market Towers, 1 Nine Elms Lane,
London SW8 5NQ
Tel: 071 627 3436

INSTITUTE OF CHARTERED ACCOUNTANTS
PO Box 433, Moorgate Place, London EC2P 2BJ
Tel: 071 628 7060

INSTITUTE OF CLERKS OF WORKS OF
GREAT BRITAIN
41 The Mall, London W5 3TJ
Tel· 081 579 2917

INSTITUTION OF CIVIL ENGINEERS
1 Great George Street, London SW1P 3AD
Tel: 071 222 7722

INSTITUTION OF ELECTRICAL ENGINEERS
Savoy Place, London WC2R 0BL
Tel: 071 240 1871

INSTITUTION OF MECHANICAL ENGINEERS
1 Birdcage Walk, London SW1X 8B11
Tel: 071 222 7899

INSTITUTION OF STRUCTURAL ENGINEERS
11 Upper Belgrave Street, London SW1X 8BH
Tel: 071 235 4535

LANDSCAPE INSTITUTE
Nash House, 12 Carlton House Terrace,
London SW1Y 5AH
Tel: 071 839 4044

LAW SOCIETY
113 Chancery Lane, London WC2A 1PL
Tel: 071 242 1222

LIBRARY ASSOCIATION
7 Ridgmount Street, London WC1E 7AE
Tel: 071 636 7543

LONDON PROPERTY REGISTER
London Residuary Body Agency Services,
County Hall, London SE1 7PB
Tel: 071 633 7494

NATIONAL COUNCIL FOR VOLUNTARY
ORGANISATIONS
26 Bedford Square, London WC1B 3HU
Tel: 071 636 4066

PLANNING AID FOR LONDON
100 Minories, London EC3N 1JY
Tel: 071 702 0051

PUBLIC RELATIONS CONSULTANTS
ASSOCIATION
Willow House, Willow Place,
London SW1P 1JH
Tel: 071 233 6026

ROYAL INSTITUTE OF BRITISH ARCHITECTS
66 Portland Place, London W1N 4AD
Tel: 071 580 5533

ROYAL INSTITUTION OF CHARTERED
SURVEYORS
12 Great George Street, London SW1P 3AD
Tel: 071 222 7000

ROYAL TOWN PLANNING INSTITUTE
26 Portland Place, London W1N 4BE
Tel: 071 636 9107

RURAL DEVELOPMENT COMMISSION
11 Cowley Street, London SW1P 3NA
Tel: 071 276 6969

SCOTTISH ARTS COUNCIL
12 Manor Place, Edinburgh EH3 7DD
Tel: 031 226 6051

SCOTTISH TOURIST BOARD
23 Ravelston Terrace, Edinburgh EH4 3EU
Tel: 031 332 2433

SPORTS COUNCIL
16 Upper Woburn Place, London WC1 H0QP
Tel: 071 388 1277

SOCIETY OF THEATRE CONSULTANTS
4 Great Pulteney Street, London W1R 0AU
Tel: 071 434 3904

THEATRES TRUST
10 St Martins Court, London WC12 4AJ
Tel: 071 836 8591

WALES TOURIST BOARD
Brunel House, 2 Fitzalan Road, Cardiff CF2 1UY
Tel:0222 499909

WELSH ARTS COUNCIL
Holst House, Museum Place, Cardiff CF1 3NX
Tel:0222 394711

REGIONAL ARTS ASSOCIATIONS
EASTERN ARTS
Cherry Hinton Hall, Cherry Hinton Road,
Cambridge CB1 4DW
Tel: 0223 215355

EAST MIDLANDS ARTS
Mountfield House, Forest Row, Loughborough,
Leicestershire LE11 3HU
Tel: 0509 218 292

GREATER LONDON ARTS
Coriander House, 20 Gainsford Street,
London SE1 2NN
Tel: 071 403 9013

LINCOLNSHIRE AND HUMBERSIDE ARTS
St Hughs, Newport, Lincoln LN1 3DN
Tel: 0522 33555

MERSEYSIDE ARTS
Graphic House, Duke Street, Liverpool L1 4JR
Tel: 051 709 0671

NORTHERN ARTS
9-10 Osbourne Terrace,
Newcastle-upon-Tyne NE2 1NZ
Tel: 091 281 6334

NORTH WEST ARTS
12 Harter Street, Manchester M1 6HY
Tel: 061 228 3062

SOUTHERN ARTS
19 Southgate Street, Winchester,
Hampshire SO23 9DQ

SOUTH EAST ARTS
10 Mount Ephraim, Tunbridge Wells,
Kent TN4 8AS
Tel: 0892 515210

SOUTH WEST ARTS
Bradninch Place, Gandy Street, Exeter EX4 3LS
Tel: 0392 218188

WEST MIDLANDS ARTS
82 Granville Street, Birmingham B1 2LH
Tel: 021 631 3121

YORKSHIRE ARTS
Glyde House, Glydegate, Bradford BD5 0BQ
Tel:0274 723051

GENERAL
Architect's appointment
Royal Institute of British Architects

Building for the Arts
Brown, Fleissig, Morrish
National Endowment for the Arts and Western
States Arts Foundation (USA)
UK Distributors: Baker and Taylor and Ingram's
Trade Publications
(Revised edition 1989)

Directory of Social Change publications
A range of publications written for voluntary organisations covering grants and fundraising,
financial management and communications.

National Council for Voluntary Organisations
publications
Books and factsheets giving information on a
range of financial, legislative and organisation
matters of interest to small organisations.

Who Does What In Europe
Arts Council (1990)

PERFORMANCE-BASED BUILDINGS
Auditoria: Design for the Performing Arts
Michael Forsyth
Batsford (1987)

Building for Music: The Architect, the Musician
and the Listener from the Seventeenth Century to
the present day
Michael Forsyth
Cambridge University Press (1985)

Detailing for Acoustics
Peter Lord and Duncan Templeton
Butterworth Architecture (1983)

'Sightline' quarterly publication, information
sheets and practice notes on specialist aspects of
theatre design
Association of British Theatre Technicians

Space for Dance: An Architectural Design Guide
Leslie Armstrong and Roger Morgan
National Endowment for the Arts (1984)

The Architecture of Sound: planning and design-
ing auditoria
Peter Lord and Duncan Templeton
Butterworth Architecture (1986)

Theatre and Playhouse
Richard and Helen Leacroft
Methuen (1984)

Theatres: Planning Guidance for Design and
Adaptation
Roderick Ham with the Association of British
Theatre Technicians
Butterworth Architecture (1987)

VISUAL ARTS
Art for Architecture. A handbook on commission-
ing sponsored by the Department of the Environ-
ment and the Calouste Gulbenkian Foundation
Edited by Deanna Petherbridge
HMSO (1987)

Arts Council Directories
Photography in the Arts Organisations and
Projects in Great Britain

On Display: A Design Grammar for Museum
Exhibitions
Margaret Hall
Lund Humphries (1987)

Organising Exhibitions
Teresa Gleadowe
Arts Council (1975)

Museum Environment and Control Preservation
Garry Thomson
Butterworth (2nd edition 1986)

ARTS CENTRE AND MIXED USE BUILDINGS
Arts Centres in the United Kingdom
Robert Hutchison and Susan Forrester
The Policy Studies Institute (1987)

Conference, Convention and Exhibition Facilities
A Handbook of Planning, Design and Manage-
ment
Fred Lawson
Architectural Press (1981)
(out of print - reprint under review)

Design for Leisure Entertainment
Anthony Wylson
Newnes and Butterworths (1980)

Getting it Together: Guidance on housing sports
and arts activities in the same building
The Sports Council in co-operation with the Arts
Council (1987)

Multi-purpose village centres: a study of their
feasibility, design and operation
Building Design Partnership and Last Suddards
& Co. for the Development Commission (1981)

Planning the Arts Centre Building
Report by Peter Eley
for the Royal Society of Arts (1986)

Public Libraries and the Arts: an evolving
partnership
Report by Peggy Heeks
Library Association (1989)

The Village Hall: Plan, Design and Build
ACRE (Action with Communities in Rural England)

Village Halls: Venues for the Arts
ACRE (planned for publication during 1991)

PLANNING AND DEVELOPMENT
An Urban Renaissance: sixteen case studies
showing the role of the arts in urban regeneration
Arts Council (1989)

Dormant Land: Wake It Up!
Department of Environment: Action for Cities
leaflet

Planning Gain
Chris Marsh
Planning Aid for London (1989)

POLICY AND MANAGEMENT
Annual Reports
Arts Council

Cultural Trends
Andrew Feist and Robert Hutchison
Policy Studies Institute

Expounding the Arts
Douglas C Mason
From research prepared for the Adam Smith
Institute (1987)

Managing the Arts: The British Experience
John Pick
Rhinegold Publishing Limited (1986)

Percent for Art
Explanatory leaflet produced by the Arts Council

Stepping Forward: Some suggestions for the
development of dance in England during the
1990s
Graham Devlin
Arts Council (1989)

Theatre is for all: Report of the Enquiry into
Professional Theatre in England
Arts Council (1986)

The Arts and Education: Policy Statement
Arts Council (1987)

The Economic Importance of the Arts in Britain
John Myerscough
The Policy Studies Institute (1988)

The Glory of the Garden
Arts Council (1985)

The Work of Art
Peter Rodgers
Policy Studies Institute (1989)

Think Rural: Act Now. A report for the Arts
Council on the arts in rural areas
Sally Stote
Arts Council (1989)

Towards Cultural Diversity
The monitoring report of the Arts Council's
ethnic minority arts action plan
Arts Council (1989)

LEGISLATION
How to Form a Company
Dennis Roberts (Revised 1986)
ICSA

Performance
Leslie E Cotterell (2nd edition)
John Offord (1984)

Practical Law for Arts Administrators
Charles Arnold Baker
John Offord (1983)

Recreation and the Law
Valerie Collins
E and F N Spon (1984)

Sponsorship of sport, arts and leisure
Stephen Townley and Edward Grayson

The Law of Public Leisure Services
Michael Scott LLM
Sweet and Maxwell (1985)

FUNDRAISING AND SOURCES OF FINANCE
A Guide to Company Giving
Edited by Michael Norton
The Directory of Social Change (1984)

A Guide to the Major Grant Making Trusts
Edited by Luke FitzHerbert
The Directory of Social Change (1986)

Company Charitable Giving: Statistics
Edited by Michael Norton
The Directory of Social Change (1987)

Directory of Grant Making Trusts
Charities Aid Foundation

Fundraising - A Comprehensive Handbook
Hilary Blume
Routlege and Kegan Paul (1977)

Fundraising and Grant Aid
Ann Darnbrough and Derek Kinrade
Woodhead-Faulkner Limited (1980)

Funds for your project. A practical guide for
Community Groups and Voluntary Organisations
The Scottish Community Education Council

Government Grants. A Guide for Voluntary
Organisations
(Revised 1988)
Compiled by Maggie Jones
Bedford Square Press for the National Council for
Voluntary Organisations

The Corporate Donors Handbook
Edited by Michael Norton
The Directory of Social Change (1987)

The Grants Register
Macmillan Publishers

DESIGNING FOR PEOPLE WITH DISABILITIES
Arts and Disability Action Plan
Arts Council (1990)
(also available on tape)

Arts and Equality: An Action Pack for Arts
Organisations
Christine S Jackson
Arts Development Association

Arts for Everyone
Anne Pearson
Carnegie UK Trust and the Centre for the
Handicapped (1985)

Designing for the Disabled (Third Edition)
Selwyn Goldsmith
RIBA Publications (1984)

The Arts and Disabilities. A Creative Response to
Social Handicap
Edited by Geoffrey Lord
Carnegie UK Trust (1982)

The Attenborough Report
Carnegie UK Trust (1985)

CONVERTING AND REFURBISHING EXISTING BUILDINGS
Building Legislation and Historic Buildings
Alan C Parnell
English Heritage and Architectural Press (1987)

Curtains!!! or A New Life For Old Theatres
The Curtains!!! Committee and individual
contributors
John Offord (1982)

Guidance notes on the repair, refurbishment and
extension of old theatre buildings
Christopher Brereton
Currently being prepared for the Theatres Trust
and English Heritage (1990)

New Uses for Older Buildings in Scotland: a
manual of practical encouragement
Scottish Civic Trust
HMSO (1981)

Re/architecture: Old Buildings/New Uses
Sherban Cantacuzino
Thames and Hudson (1989)

Re-using Redundant Buildings: Good practice in
urban regeneration
Department of the Environment with URBED
(Urban and Economic Development Ltd.) (1987)

Reviving Buildings and Communities: a manual of
renewal
Michael Talbot
David & Charles (1987)

INDEX

Erratum Sheet

1. In November 1990 the Minister for the Arts asked the Arts Council to replace its Incentive Funding Scheme with an Enhancement Fund to strengthen selected, leading arts organisations. This means that the introduction of the Council's Capital Fund and of the Arts Council Television, both of which are referred to several times in the book, has had to be postponed.

2. Expanded information on four sections in Appendix 2 (pp 105 - 6) is outlined below:

THE HOME OFFICE MANUAL
Guide to Fire Precautions in Existing Places of Entertainment and Like Premises. (Available from HMSO.)

A fully revised version was published in 1990. It is advisory only, and applies to existing buildings. It is not intended as a design guide for new buildings – that is the function of BS 5588 Pt. 6. It will therefore not be superseded by the new British Standard.

There are unfortunately some differences between the two documents e.g. in the way exits' widths are calculated, and the introduction to the Home Office Manual makes clear that a building designed in accordance with the British Standard will be acceptable when it becomes an 'existing building' after completion.

The Home Office Manual is an important document because it is readily available to Fire Officers who are consulted about licensing arts buildings for public use.

GREATER LONDON COUNCIL REGULATIONS AND RULES
The widely respected GLC Rules of Management and Technical Regulations are now out of date, although still much used as a reference. (Copies are still available from the ABTT.)

To avoid confusion, when entertainment licensing was transferred to the London Boroughs, the London District Surveryor's Association undertook to revise and re-issue the Rules of Management and Technical Regulations. They have now issued model Rules of Management (available from LDSA Publications, P.O. Box 710, London SW18 4JS) and the Technical Regulations are in preparation. No authority is bound by these new rules, but they are being widely adopted in London, and it is to be hoped the rest of the country will follow.

BRITISH STANDARDS
BS 5588   Fire Precautions in the Design, Construction and Use of Buildings.
Part 6   Code of Practice for Places of Assembly.

This part, long in preparation, will be published by Easter 1991. A final draft is complete.

As each successive part of BS 5588 is published, the Department of the Environment refers to it in revisions of the Building Regulations, thus giving it the force of law.For this reason BS 5588 Pt. 6 is a most important and influential document, which will shape any arts building for public use.

ACCESS FOR THE DISABLED
The building Regulations Part M gives details of access requirements.

BS 5588 Part 8: 1988 is the Code of Practice for Means of Escape for Disabled People.
(British Standards available from BSI, Linford Wood, Milton Keynes, MK14 6LE.)

16th January 1991.